P9-CNF-407

# Check Your Discipleship

by
Knofel
Staton

New Life
BOOKS™

A division of STANDARD PUBLISHING
Cincinnati, Ohio
39991

ISBN: 0-87239-424-7

## Dedication

To the two who are great in-laws to me and fantastic
grandparents to Randy, Rena, Rhonda, and Rachel—
Ralph and Helen Coons

## Appreciation

No book is done by me apart from others. I particu-
larly want to thank Julia for typing the original manu-
script from my handwriting and Marilyn Smith and
Jeaneane Chaney for doing the final copy.

## Table of Contents

# CHAPTER ONE

# MIMICKING THE MASTER

We are all disciples of someone, and we all have those who are our disciples. The mother who has a little tot standing on a chair beside her as she bakes cookies has a disciple in that child. The intern in the hospital who is learning the practical aspects of medicine is a disciple of the medical doctors. The apprentice who is assigned to learn from a master craftsman is a disciple of that craftsman. And each of these disciples is trying to mimic his leader.

As a part of Jesus' ministry on earth, He selected twelve men to become His disciples. While He ministered to the needs of the many, He spent His few years as a minister and teacher discipling a small number of men. Because of this discipling method, Christianity did not retreat when the Master was no longer on earth. Instead, within a decade it mushroomed to a number that no man could count. Jesus left disciples for His church who filled a purpose, not just attenders who filled pews. And He made clear that we are to continue making disciples.

But we are not to make just any disciples. Every philosopher in the first century had a group of disciples who followed him. Every political leader had disciples.

In the New Testament we read about the disciples of John the Baptist (Matthew 9:14; 11:2; 14:12), the disciples of the Pharisees (Matthew 22:16—God forbid that we make such disciples today!), and disciples of Paul (Acts 9:25). Our goal, however, is to make disciples of *Jesus,* just as John and Paul pointed their disciples to Jesus (John 1:29-31; 1 Corinthians 11:1).

But who is a disciple of Jesus and how do we make one? Without a clear picture of our objective we will spin our wheels, use up our time and energy, and still not make any disciples. We can lose much time by trying the trial-and-error way to find the right discipling formula. Instead, let us look to Jesus and His methods.

## THE MENTALITY

Jesus was intent upon making disciples, not in drawing crowds. And there is a difference. Many packaged programs in the church may draw crowds but not make disciples of Jesus.

I was in a church not long ago that had the reputation of being an active church. The preacher had built the attendance by using gimmicks. But when he left, the crowds left also. Only a handful of people remained. The church was then known in the community for its bickering and meanness. Immorality was common among the members, and everyone knew it. The preacher had brought the crowds, but he had not made disciples of Jesus.

Crowds can be built by sheer accident. Watch what happens when two automobiles crash. A crowd forms. But disciples of Jesus are never made by accident. That takes planning and purpose.

Crowds can be built on the basis of provided entertainment. Watch the crowds gather when a music

6

group comes to town. But providing entertainment will not make disciples of Jesus. Enlightenment is what is needed.

There is nothing wrong with drawing crowds to the place where we worship and study about God and His Son Jesus. That's great! If you are doing that, keep it up. But don't think the job is finished when the crowds have shown up for the special attraction. The real job has just begun. The fatiguing work zeros in on what to do after the crowd has come—*and* after it has left.

Jesus drew crowds. On one occasion He had a crowd of 5,000 men plus women and children. Wouldn't it be great to have 5,000 men in the audience *with* their families? What an opportunity! But we must not just count them. They must count.

Jesus performed a crowd-pleasing feat when he fed them all (probably 10,000-12,000 people). Of course, the crowds returned the next day. But Jesus would not feed them that day. He knew that if the only reason they gathered was to get a free meal, then the meal would become their master and not He.

He started teaching them a disciple-making lesson. But many walked out on the lesson. They wanted food, not faith; loaves, not love; gifts, not demands. Jesus let the crowds leave (John 6:66). Would we do that? It depends on whether we see that the Great Commission says, "Go to the world and make crowds" or, "Go to the world and make disciples."

We have so long fed upon the crowd mentality that often we cannot tell the difference between the crowds and the disciples. The people in the New Testament could tell the difference. Several times we read about the presence of both the disciples and the crowd (Mark 3:7; 9:14; Luke 6:17; Acts 19:9).

7

Don't misunderstand me. I am not pushing for a program of smallness. The church has glorified smallness too long. Sometimes Christians seem to think there is something wrong with God's being able to draw a multitude. Our God is interested in the *whole* world. Nothing smaller than that is His target. When the church first began, three thousand people were baptized (Acts 2:41). That is hardly showing that "smaller is better." Jesus said, "Make disciples of all nations" (Matthew 28:19). We should not feel we have finished the race when our buildings are 90 percent full and we need two worship services to accommodate the members.

Still, God is not interested in a flash-in-the-pan program that draws crowds but does not produce disciples. He does not want programs that just hook the people and then leave them dangling on the line. He wants faithful disciples that can lead the crowds to Jesus—disciples who have been fed and trained.

Another problem that goes along with the crowd mentality is our desire for "instant" everything. We want to make "instant" disciples of Jesus along with our instant tea, coffee, rice, and mashed potatoes. We are in as much a hurry to make disciples of Jesus as the auto industry has been to make automobiles. No wonder when our "instant" disciples get off the "assembly line," they often break down. Look in any junk yard, and you will see the results of the instant, mass production of automobiles. By the same token look at the inactive list in any church membership book, and you will see the results of attempting to produce "instant" disciples of Jesus. God does not want "instant" discipleship; He wants the stability of a mature faith that comes with patient teaching.

## THE DEFINITION

To understand Jesus' way of making disciples, let us look very closely at the meaning of the phrase "making disciples."

*Directing the Mind.* The Greek word from which this phrase comes has an interesting history. *Matheteuo* literally means "to direct one's mind to something." Making disciples involves the process of directing people's minds to whatever we want them to become disciples of. A disciple in the field of medicine spends time in the hospital, talks with doctors and other medical personnel, and studies from books about medicine. He does all this to fill his mind with medical knowledge.

There can be no such person as a disciple of Jesus who does not have his mind fixed on *Jesus.* A disciple of Jesus must seek to have his mind filled with the thoughts and teachings of Jesus. It is no surprise that many pulpits have this saying burned into the wood, "We would see Jesus." Maybe those of us who seek to disciple others should have that same motto burned into our minds.

*Getting Accustomed.* Not only is the mind to be directed toward Jesus, but the person is to get accustomed to Jesus' way. To what are we getting people accustomed? Games, gimmicks, sensational attractions, emotional displays, entertainment—or to Jesus? Whatever we hook people *with* is what they will become disciples *of.* We want people to get accustomed to Jesus' attitudes, actions, and reactions. We hope they will get accustomed to Jesus' mind-set as they learn lessons from the Bible and as they see His lifestyle imitated in our lives.

*Entering an Experience.* Discipleship does not stop

with the directing of one's mind or with getting him accustomed to Jesus' ways. It also involves entering into the experience of living the Christian life. I would never have become a disciple of air traffic control if someone had not handed me the microphone and said, "Start controlling." No intern can become a doctor just by watching other doctors perform; part of his training must be actually diagnosing sicknesses and treating patients. At the same time we cannot expect a person to be a disciple of Jesus just by having a perfect attendance record at church and Sunday school. We cannot reduce discipleship to pew-sitting. A disciple of Jesus is actively applying Jesus' life and teachings to his own life.

A disciple of Jesus does not learn simply to know something. Having a photographic memory and making straight A's in Bible memory work do not equal being a disciple of Jesus. It has been reported that Hitler had memorized the four Gospels word for word, but he certainly was not a disciple of Jesus.

A disciple learns in order to *do.* He learns in order to *follow.* Learning and living go hand in hand for the disciple of Jesus. He learns in order to *mimic* what He has learned. Paul expressed this concept when he called people to imitate him just as he imitated (mimicked) Christ (1 Corinthians 11:1). He pointed to Christ as our model and made clear that a disciple of Christ will produce Christlikeness in his own life.

Several years ago, when I was visiting a Buddhist temple in Bangkok, I purchased a rubbing made by some Thai people. We struck up a friendly conversation, after which they took me behind the scenes to show me how they made the rubbings. The process was a simple one. They placed a piece of material over

10

an engraved image on the wall of the temple and started to rub until the image on the wall was reproduced onto the material. It was the same process that we used as children when we would put a penny under a piece of paper and rub over the paper until the image of the penny apeared on the paper.

Becoming a disciple of Jesus is a similar process. A disciple will so expose the material of his total life to Jesus that Jesus' life-style will become his and Jesus' image will be seen in him. The disciple of Jesus is the learned follower who mimics His Master.

When we become a disciple of Jesus, we come down the aisle singing, "Just as I am, I come." But we go back up that aisle saying, "Just as He is, so I will become."

## PROGRESSING TOWARD THE GOAL

The New Testament makes clear God's goal for us: God has "predestined [us] to be conformed to the likeness of his Son . . ." (Romans 8:29). Paul said that God has given the church various kinds of leaders "to prepare God's people for works of service, so that the body of Christ may be built up until we all reach unity in the faith and in the knowledge of the Son of God and become mature, attaining to the whole measure of the fullness of Christ" (Ephesians 4:12, 13).

We are to grow to become just like Christ. Paul committed himself to bringing disciples of Christ to total Christlikeness: "We proclaim him, admonishing and teaching everyone with all wisdom, so that we may present everyone perfect in Christ" (Colossians 1:28). The word *perfect* means mature. It is the same word that is translated "mature" in Ephesians 4:13, where it clearly means attaining Christlikeness.

Jesus selected His disciples and taught them so they could become like Him: "A student is not above his teacher, but everyone who is fully trained will be like his teacher" (Luke 6:40). A faithful disciple will seek to become like his teacher.

But becoming like Jesus takes time. It is not an activity that can be reserved for Sundays only. Disciples of Jesus will be progressing *daily* toward maturity in Christ (2 Corinthians 3:18).

Jesus' disciples are becomers. We are unfinished products. There is the "now" and the "not yet" aspect in each one of us. We are now disciples of Jesus, but we are not yet fully what we shall become. Each disciple could have these letters engraved on his life: H P W M F G I N F W M Y. What do they mean? "Have patience with me, for God is not finished with me yet."

John wrote, "We know that when he appears, we shall be like him . . ." (1 John 3:2). But we are not to sit around and twiddle our thumbs, waiting for Christ-likeness to descend upon us. The disciple of Jesus who hopes to be like Jesus *then* is doing something about it *now.* John used the Greek word *kathos,* which means "just as" (translated in the NIV as "shall be like"), referring to exact correspondence. As we search for other Scriptures that use this word, we can find many ways the true disciple of Jesus is to be "just as" Jesus is.

The disciple is to be "just as" Jesus (God) is in his
    Walk (1 John 2:6)
    Purity (1 John 3:2, 3)
    Righteousness (1 John 3:7)
    Love (1 John 3:23; John 13:34)
    Life-style (1 John 4:17)
    Conduct (John 13:15, 34; 15:12)
    Unity (John 17:11, 21)

12

Mercy (Luke 6:36)
Forgiveness
(Ephesians 4:32; Colossians 3:13)
Love for the church
(Ephesians 5:25)

Using the above list and the points in the following chapters, we can check our personal discipleship as well as evaluate our ministries for others. Are the lives of those whom we touch by our teaching or witnessing becoming like Christ? An unknown author expressed the thought well:

> Measure your success as teachers not by the size of your audience, which may after all be only a huge ecclesiastical jellyfish, drifting aimlessly and uselessly through the social sea, but by the stature and dimension of the manhood which you develop in individual believers, by the orderliness and service-ableness and Christ-likeness of the separate disciple whom you build into the Christian brotherhood.

# CHAPTER TWO

# THE MODEL DISCIPLE

It takes a true disciple to make a true disciple. When Jesus called men to become His disciples, He did not call them to become something He himself was not, for discipleship can also be described as sonship. It is not difficult to see the parallel between the father-son relationship and the teacher-disciple relationship in our lives as well as in the family of God.

Jesus existed as a coequal with the Father prior to His coming to earth (Philippians 2:6; John 17:5); but when He came to earth, He humbled himself and became a servant-son (Philippians 2:7, 8). In that sonship, He was the perfect disciple. Thus, by looking at His life, we can know what a true disciple is to be.

## HUMILITY

Jesus began His life in humility. He could have demanded the best since His Father was the world's creator and owner, but He didn't. He didn't feel cheated by being born to a poor family. He wasn't bothered by the fact that He had the finest mind in the land, but spent many of His days working as a lowly carpenter. He was not ashamed to do manual labor.

Athough He owned the cattle on a thousand hills, He evidently never claimed one as His own while He was on earth. He did not own a place to be born in or a place in which to be buried. He never owned a home, but rested in the homes of friends. He did not own a donkey and had to borrow one when He chose not to walk.

Thus He was not being hypocritical when He declared, "In the same way, any of you who does not give up everything he has cannot be my disciple" (Luke 14:33). He did not mean that each disciple had to sell everything he owned, for Jesus' disciples did not do that. But He did mean that His disciples must mentally "give up" everything to the ownership of God, who allows us to be His stewards. It is the attitude that all that we have is God's and can be used to serve Him. And if there is a need to do so, all can be given away. The real disciple would feel no pangs of regret in doing so, for he would be giving back to God what had been entrusted to him for a short time. He would have much the same feeling as a friend who borrows your car, uses it for a while, and then returns it to you (its owner) when the time comes.

## FREEDOM

Jesus was reared in a great home. Joseph and Mary were willing to be misunderstood and maligned for Jesus' sake. After all, how many people would really believe that the Holy Spirit made Mary pregnant? And just as Joseph was probably getting settled in a job at Bethlehem, he was willing to leave it to move to a foreign land to protect the child. How many people today give the welfare of their children the first priority in deciding where they will live? Joseph and Mary also made sure Jesus was exposed to the religious festivals in Jerusalem as soon as He was old enough to participate. Yes, His family members were considerate and were concerned about the needs of one another.

With such family life often comes a natural reluctance to break family ties. Jesus could have been pleasingly secure if He had stayed home. But when the time was right, He left. He walked away from the family business and the family ties. He freed himself to become involved in God's business.

There comes a time in every person's life when he must break away from his parents and become a disciple of Jesus. Jesus taught, "If anyone comes to me and does not hate his father and mother, his wife and children, his brothers and sisters—yes, even his own life—he cannot be my disciple" (Luke 14:26). The word for "hate" that Jesus used does not just mean "despise." He was not saying we must despise our families. In other teachings He made it clear that we are always to respect our mothers and fathers (Matthew 15:3-9). The Greek word for "hate" also meant giving second priority to something. Jesus was saying that a disciple of His must be free from seeking to please his family first or making his family the first priority in his life. Many who wanted to be Jesus' disciples could not fulfill this task (Luke 9:57-62).

Jesus called some of His first disciples to leave their family business and follow Him (Matthew 4:18-22). Could they do it? It was a real test of discipleship. A disciple of Jesus cannot be tied to worldly possessions or considerations; He must be free to serve and follow.

## PATIENCE

Jesus knew that He had come to care for the unlovely, demonstrate the character of God, destroy the works of the devil, and save the world. There must have been many times that He wanted to say to the Father, "Now, Father, let's do it now." He must have

16

ached to touch the leper, heal the blind child, or raise the invalid father so he could provide for his family. But as a disciple, He knew He must do things in God's time.

Jesus waited thirty years to begin His ministry. After He called His disciples, they had to wait a year before they received their first assignment. After He arose from the grave and appeared to His disciples, they were ready to rush out and tell the world about Jesus. But at that point, Jesus gave them a tough commandment. He told them to go to Jerusalem and *wait*. What? Yes, wait!

A disciple of Jesus must learn not to be impetuous or run ahead of Jesus. We must learn to wait. We must wait for people to mature; they are not able to mature overnight. If we become impatient with others, we may discourage them rather than encourage them. We must learn to wait for the planted seed of evangelism to yield fruit. We must not cut people off too early, or they may never become Christians. We must learn to wait for the second coming. If we can't, then when the pressures of life on earth continue to build, we may become too discouraged to remain His disciples.

We must learn to wait for God's vengeance to make things right. We must not rush out and try to do so ourselves, for then we would be repaying evil with evil. We must learn to wait for recognition and rewards. If we can't, we may become sidetracked by instant applause. We may replace the service of discipleship with seeking for its status, and thus replace interest in Jesus with interest in self.

## OBEDIENCE

It may seem odd to say that Jesus learned while He

was on earth, but He did. He learned what every disciple must learn. He learned to obey (Hebrews 5:8). Obedience is not a natural flow from humans. We *learn* to obey. It is one of the most important things we can learn, for what good is it to learn facts if we don't obey? What good is it to memorize Scripture if we don't apply it?

There is no such thing as discipleship apart from obedience, for it provides the abiding commitment that is at the very center of discipleship. Jesus said, "If you hold to my teaching, you are really my disciples" (John 8:31). And there is no substitute for obedience. We either obey or we don't.

An obedient disciple follows his teacher. Jesus learned to be a good follower before He became the leader of followers. As a boy He declared, "Didn't you know I had to be in my Father's house?" (Luke 2:49). And as an adult He said, "For I have come down from heaven not to do my will but to do the will of him who sent me" (John 6:38).

"A student is not above his teacher . . ." (Luke 6:40). Who was Jesus' teacher while He was on earth? God was. And Jesus followed His teacher with such dedication that He admitted He did not say or do anything on His own initiative: "By myself I can do nothing" (John 5:30); ". . . I do nothing on my own but speak just what the Father has taught me" (John 8:28).

## SERVICE

Jesus was a servant of God for the people. He came to meet needs. If someone was hungry, Jesus fed him. If someone was lonely, Jesus was his friend. If someone was rejected, Jesus accepted him. If someone had sinned, Jesus forgave him. The disciple who traveled with Him soon learned that a disciple of His was to be a servant of God for the benefit of others.

Jesus was not an isolationist. He put himself into the middle of the arena where the people were. He practiced friendship evangelism wrapped up in the package of compassionate care. He was God's "CARE package" to the world.

It is not possible for one of Jesus' disciples to be a spiritual ostrich by keeping his head in the sand and not be involved in the world. Jesus called His disciples to work and to serve (Matthew 20:25-28), and He expected them to go into the world (Matthew 28:19), not to separate themselves from the world. On the night He was betrayed, He prayed that His disciples would not isolate themselves from the world, "My prayer is not that you take them out of the world but that you protect them from the evil one" (John 17:15). We need insulation against the onslaughts of the world, not isolation.

## REPRESENTATION

Jesus was the exact representation of God (Hebrews 1:3). As God in flesh (John 1:1, 14), He was the "image of the invisible God" (Colossians 1:15). When people saw Him, they saw God in action; for Jesus came to make God known (John 1:18). He said, "Anyone who has seen me has seen the Father" (John 14:9).

A disciple of Jesus is to live in such a way that people can see Jesus through him. That is one reason the church is called the body of Christ. As a body allows the person to be visible, disciples allow Christ to be viewed. To represent Jesus really means to represent Him—to present Him again. It is no wonder that Jesus said to His disciples, "Let your light shine before men, that they may see your good deeds and praise your Father in heaven" (Matthew 5:16).

## PRAYERFULNESS

Jesus was a man of prayer. He stayed in communication with His Father-Teacher. He would rise up early in the morning to pray (Mark 1:35); He prayed during the day (Luke 5:16). Sometimes He prayed all night (Luke 6:12); He prayed before meals (Matthew 14:19), with adults and children (Matthew 19:13), after strenuous activity (Matthew 14:23), while engaged in something that was spiritually significant (Luke 3:21), in crowds, and by himself (Luke 9:18). Sometimes He left the multitudes in order to pray. At other times He even got away from His disciples in order to pray (Mark 6:46). It was not unusual for the disciples to start looking for Him—and then find Him praying alone (Mark 1:36, 37).

The disciples noticed His prayerfulness and asked Him to teach them to pray. In fact, that is the only thing they asked Him to teach them. They knew that effective discipleship must include regular praying.

## GROWTH

Jesus was not always as mature as we see Him during His ministry. He was once a child and "grew in wisdom and stature, and in favor with God and men" (Luke 2:52).

A disciple of Jesus must not have the philosophy that "I've never been like that, and I can't change now." One of the beautiful things about eleven of the twelve disciples was that they did change. The one who did not change soon discovered that life was not worth living for him.

As we were born to grow physically, so we are born again to grow spiritually. To get stuck in the mud of sameness is a tragedy and will not result in true discipleship of Christ. Anyone who is the same this year as he was last year should repent. A person who will not change is setting himself up as one who is infallible and thus is a competitor to God, not God's companion and servant, and certainly not Christ's disciple.

## RIGHTEOUSNESS

Jesus was tempted in every way any human being was and is, but He did not sin (Hebrews 4:15). After more than thirty years of life, not one charge of immoral or dishonest activity could be made against Him. His life was characterized by impeccability.

A disciple of Jesus must hunger and thirst for righteousness (Matthew 5:6). Hungering and thirsting are strong words. A starving person is not picky, nor does he add to the menu. He dreams about food, he puts forth the effort to find food, and will eat when the food is available. In the same way a person who truly hungers after righteousness will not only *say* he wants righteousness, but he will also *do everything* in his power to attain it.

Not only did Jesus love and seek after what was good, but He also hated what was evil. We hear much about what and who God loves, but we hear very little about what and who God hates. God does hate. He hates all evil. And Jesus loved what God loved and hated what He hated. (God can hate people: Proverbs 6:16-19).

A disciple of Jesus will also hate. Paul wrote that

followers of Jesus should "hate what is evil" (Romans 12:9). Do you hate evil? Do you spend your evenings watching all the evil portrayed on television? How can a person who gets his kicks from watching people fight, yell, rape, stab, and kill claim to be a disciple of Jesus? Can you imagine Jesus watching such things every night—or *any* night?

## COMMITMENT

Jesus never yielded even an inch in His commitment. He resisted all the devil's attempts to detour His mission (Matthew 4). He rejected the crowds when they tried to turn Him away from His mission. He would not allow His friends or His disciples to talk Him out of going to the cross. And He didn't allow His enemies to scare Him.

Nowhere do we see His commitment put to the test more vividly than in the Garden of Gethsemane on the night He was betrayed. His feelings were crying out, "Let's not go through with this." Three times He prayed, "If it is possible, let this cup pass from me." If Jesus had lived His life based on His feelings, as many modern-day Christians like to do, He would never have gone to the cross. We are all quite fortunate and blessed that His commitment and responsibilities were more important to Him than His feelings of the moment. This commitment cost Him His life.

Denying self and cross-bearing are to be the characteristics of all disciples of Jesus. In fact , no one can be called a true disciple without the attitude of self-sacrifice and being determined to fulfill commitments. For Jesus said, "If anyone would come after me, he must deny himself and take up his cross and follow me" (Matthew 16:24).

22

## SUMMARY

Do you really want to be a disciple of Jesus? Then remember that He is the model disciple, and He portrayed for us very clearly what the life and attitudes of a disciple are to be. If we are to be His disciples, we must seek to mimic Him in every area of life. We must direct our minds to Him, get accustomed to Him, enter His experience, and duplicate His life-style. All of this means we will put the following ingredients into our lives:

> Humility
> Freedom
> Patience
> Obedience
> Service
> Representation
> Prayerfulness
> Growth
> Righteousness
> Commitment

# CHAPTER THREE

# SELECTING THE DISCIPLES

**THE NEED**

Jesus knew that in three years He would no longer be on the earth in His physical body. Would the work that He started be strong enough to continue without His physical presence? How could it go on?

Jesus' plan to continue and expand His work involved discipled people—men molded into His likeness, not molded by the world. But that meant that He would have to invest much time with His disciples, for people cannot be discipled without guidance, correction, fellowship, and involvement with Him. Jesus knew that a handful of committed disciples would do more to win the world and maintain His mission than millions of uncommitted people would do.

Within fifty days after His death only one hundred twenty disciples were meeting together (Acts 1:15; there may have been more disciples than met on this occasion, see 1 Corinthians 15:6, but we don't really know). That doesn't seem like an impressive number for the miracle-working, charismatic, dynamic speaker and leader that Jesus was. That number represents a possibility of Jesus' winning only forty people per year in His ministry. Such a record would get many preachers fired today; they would be called lazy and ineffective. We are quick to count numbers and let that be the criteria for success. But we need to consider *what* we are counting. The number one hundred twenty may not be impressive if you are counting pennies; it would be more impressive if you were counting dollar bills, and even more so if you were counting million-dollar bills! In the same way, one hundred twenty people may not sound like many for three years of work until we realize that those people were faithful, committed *disciples* who had been with Jesus. That kind of people could carry on His work.

Just think of the accomplishments of these few disciples, and compare them with the accomplishments of the many curiosity-seekers that thronged Jesus when He fed them the bread and fishes. You will see one major difference between a crowd and disciples. What the crowd did was discussed within just a few short verses, but notice how much of the Bible covered the activities of these few disciples! I wonder how big a book would need to be written to cover all the accomplishments of each of those disciples. Few people would be able to lift such a book, and certainly no one would be able to study all its pages even in a lifetime.

Those few disciples multiplied to three thousand on the Day of Pentecost (Acts 2:41), then to five thousand (4:4), then to a number no man could count. That was a high return for Jesus' investment in just a few. What a difference commitment makes!

## THE DRAFT

If we want to enlist people to do a task today, we often simply call for volunteers and then wonder why people are not crowding the aisles to help us out.

Jesus did not ask for volunteers. Instead He looked over the people, considered their potential, considered the task to be done, and then began choosing those He wanted to fulfill the task. On the night He was betrayed, He reminded them, "You did not choose me, but I chose you . . ." (John 15:16).

Jesus chose people to be His disciples with a two-fold invitation that included privilege and purpose. He appointed twelve to be with Him (privilege) and to be sent out to preach (purpose, Mark 3:14). He promised no door prizes; He put no dollar bills underneath the seats on the bus; He promised no one riches. His invitation was not flowery or flattering; He got right to the point and called for a radical obedience. When Jesus called James, John, Peter, and Andrew, they were at their place of business and were highly involved; but Jesus told them to follow Him and change their business (Mark 1:17). He promised them nothing but himself (privilege) and a job (purpose). How did they react to such a tough request? "At once they left their nets and followed Him" (Mark 1:18-20).

We do people an injustice when we do not lay all the aspects of God's call face-up on the table. Too often we tell people about all the privileges, but keep the purpose aspect hidden until after they decide to follow Jesus. We dangle the privileges in front of them and then wonder why they balk when we later expect purposeful activity from them. We change the rules in the middle of the game—why shouldn't they resist? People deserve to know at the outset that there is service involved in discipleship. Not only must they realize the great gift from God; they must also realize the cost of commitment.

Perhaps we think people will shrink from the idea of

26

service and responsibility. But most people are seeking for purpose in their lives, and Jesus does all of us a favor by calling us to fulfill responsibilities. Psychologist Gordon Allport maintains that every person is an adolescent psychologically until he has a definite objective—a goal in which he loses himself for another (see *Patterns and Growth in Personality,* Holt, Rinehart, and Winston, 1937). Another psychologist, William Glasser (see *Reality Therapy,* Harper & Row, 1965), is getting at the same principle when he teaches that humans get into trouble when their performance is too low. He says that one of the basic needs of man is the need to be functionally responsible. He suggests that we have been too quick to blame irresponsibility on mental illness. The truth is that man is not irresponsible because he is mentally ill; man is mentally ill because he remains irresponsible.

A person's better nature becomes apparent when he has a purpose bigger than himself to reach for. That is the reason Jesus' disciples shone so greatly. Jesus gave them a purpose bigger than they were. And even though they were unlikely men to become great, their lights were the brightest. All they needed was to have their lights turned on.

Is it possible that people leave the church not because the church asks too much of them but because it asks too little? Is it possible that people can use their talents for the company only to see them buried in the church? Perhaps we often do not trust people with responsibility in the church. The company may trust a person with a million-dollar budget, but at church the board has to approve his spending ten dollars. We must begin to trust and free people so they can do something in and for the church.

## THE DIVERSITY

Jesus did not select His disciples by using a cookie cutter. He called people who were very different, and He honored those differences. It is a part of God's creative will that people are different.

No two people are exactly alike. Each of us is unique. God has stamped individuality upon each one of us. No two fingerprints are alike. No two voices are alike. Even the texture of each person's hair is different. Each person receives a half cell from his father and a half cell from his mother. In that cell are the genetic codes of all of our past ancestors and the combination of our potential characteristics, including height, hair color, and eye color. A person born today could become one of 250 plus 240 billion zeroes genetic combinations. If a person spent eight hours a day for five days a week writing down that large a number, it would take him forty-five years just to write the zeros.

Jesus did not expect His disciples to be alike. Some were men; some were women (Luke 8:3). Some were rich; some were poor. Some were respected people (Joseph of Arimathea, Matthew 27:57); some had tainted reputations prior to their discipleship (woman at the well, John 4). But they all learned what it meant to be Jesus' disciples. They learned about commitment and its cost.

We are probably missing out on some of the most creative and productive disciples by deciding ahead of time who is and who is not good discipleship material. *Everyone* is discipleship material because Jesus came for the whole world. Some of the most unlikely (in our view) people can become dynamic disciples. They are just waiting for someone to light their fuses.

One such person is Jack McCoy. On the outside, he

seems unassuming and is not impressive. He is an official in a tire plant. One night a week he drove thirty miles to take a class in a seminary where I taught. He made it a habit to come an hour or two earlier so he could talk to me in my study. He wanted to talk about how he could live out his discipleship at work.

One day Jack sent a memo throughout the plant that he would start a Bible study in his office. When the first session was to start, so many people showed up that he had to borrow a bigger office. Within two months, he had five different Bible studies going. Before long some members of the union filed an official grievance about the Bible studies. What was their complaint? They were upset because the Bible studies were available for shifts one and two but not for shift three!

During this period came the time for the annual plant inspection by the central office. Of course, the inspectors discovered the active Bible studies. The inspection report noted the marked change of morale throughout the plant and concluded that the Bible studies made the difference. The inspectors recommended that the home office require availability of Bible studies in each of their plants across the nation.

Jack not only affected people in these groups; he also reached out to individuals personally. Ed was married with six kids and worked at the plant. He was a good artist and was regularly putting his artwork of "not-so-nice" pictures on the bulletin boards at the plant. Jack wanted to reach Ed for Christ and decided to do so through his interest in art. Jack asked him to draw a picture of what he thought Hell looked like. Jack said, "You have never seen such a scary picture." He then asked Ed to draw a picture that would show the difference in a man when he became a Christian—a before and after picture. On one side of the paper Ed drew a man sitting on a stool in a room with the plaster falling down and a single light bulb hanging from the ceiling. The man's body was facing outward, but his face turned toward the wall. He was too ashamed to look at people. On the other side of the paper was the same man standing straight, his face looking outward with a big smile. Not only had he changed on the inside; he had also changed on the outside. His clothes and environment were different. Christ had made him new. Ed was catching on to what discipleship meant.

Eventually the "not-so-nice" pictures were not appearing on the bulletin boards any more. Jack invited me to speak in his church one Sunday, and whom did I see filling one pew? Ed, his wife, and their six children!

God can use us no matter who we are. We don't have to be a Jack McCoy. He can also use a Nellie Matthews. Nellie was probably the oldest person in our church. At least as a boy growing up, I thought she was. Nellie was stooped over at a 45-degree angle; she could not look up to see anyone's face. She always wore black, and she would shake constantly. But every time the church building was open, Nellie Matthews was there. She would walk through snow, ice, wind, and driving rain to get there. She always sat on the end of the fourth pew on the right.

Although she never knew it, she ministered to me when I was in Korea during the war. After a close encounter with death, every time I thought of my hometown church I pictured Nellie Matthews sitting in the fourth pew on the right. I did not realize as I was growing up what an indelible impression her faithfulness had made upon me, but in Korea during those dangerous times I thought that if Christianity was so important to her in those latter days of her life when she was feeble and sick, then Christianity must be important to me as a young lad far away from home. Nellie Matthews helped me to remain faithful. When I think of her, I think about Jesus' words when He spoke of a woman in His day, "She did what she could . . ." (Mark 14:8). That is a mark of discipleship—doing what we can.

Another real disciple is Julia Scott. She is a widow in her late sixties. She has always been service-oriented and wondered what she could do for Christ. She looked at her abilities as a former nurse and decided that she could help unfortunate children. She became a foster mother. She would care for the babies that no one wanted.

Iscah was a physical mess when Julia took her. She was illegitimate, deformed, and unwanted. She was born without a rectum and with many other irregularities in her inner organs. She had over twenty surgeries in her first few years of life. All of the surgery had to be done in Columbia, Missouri, two hundred miles away from Carthage, Julia's home. Julia spent most of her days in the hospital being a loving mother to Iscah. Every Sunday the baby was able, Julia and Iscah were in church. Iscah became a lovable, pretty, smiling little girl. When she was three, a couple from St. Louis wanted her for their own. Little Iscah now has a bright future because the disciple Julia cared and reached out in love.

Yes, the disciples of Jesus are varied, but they all learn and live out the commitment that Jesus expects.

31

## THE DENIALS

Jesus did not accept all those who said they wanted to be His disciples. Too many people wanted to be on His bandwagon, but they had no intention of fulfilling His purposes.

Once an extremely rich young ruler came to Jesus. But Jesus let him walk away. Discipleship involves being willing to give away everything you own; but that young man, though very moral and sincere, was not willing to pay the price for discipleship (Luke 18:18-23).

On another occasion, Jesus allowed multitudes of people to walk away because they wanted only the *privileges* of discipleship (John 6). This does not mean once rejected always rejected. But it does mean that Jesus expects us to be serious about following Him. We cannot come to Jesus on any other terms than those He has laid down—submissiveness and obedience. Any other way would lead to our trying to master Him rather than letting Him master us.

The people in John 6 tried to manipulate Jesus. They tried to squeeze Him into their mold of who they thought He ought to be and how they wanted Him to act. They wanted to make Him over so He could fit nicely into their way of life. Their idea was, "We will let you be our king as long as we can write up the planks of your platform." They did not want a Lord to serve; they wanted an eternal Santa Claus to give them goodies. Jesus refused those who were only interested in the goodies.

It is too easy to live for self and in that way lose the self we are living for. That is why Jesus did not accept all who wanted to jump on His bandwagon. He wanted those who were willing to live lives of lowly service for others. Jesus knew He would soon be on His way to Jerusalem to be executed. He knew that life would be extremely difficult for His disciples then. He would need followers who had pure commitments and whose eyes were wide open to the problems they would have to face. He did not want men who could be swept away by His sensational miracles or who would make rash promises they were not willing to carry out.

One person told Jesus, "I will follow you wherever you go." Sounds like a wonderful type of surrender, doesn't it? Jesus wants us to surrender ourselves, but not blindly. This person did not know that Jesus was headed for Calvary or that He was going to receive a cross, not a crown.

For this reason, Jesus proceeded to make this person aware of what commitment to Him really meant, "The foxes have holes, and the birds of the air have nests, but the Son of Man has nowhere to lay His head" (Luke 9:58, NASB). Jesus made clear that possessions and riches do not come automatically when one becomes His disciple. Real commitment involves counting the cost, not the cash. It calls for denial of self, not just the delights of success. One who wants to be committed to Jesus must be willing to give away all he has, not to be out there grabbing for all he can get (Luke 14:33; Matthew 19:21). Jesus was saying, "I have produced miracles; but if you follow me, don't expect me to produce your every material whim."

Jesus was also emphasizing the danger that lies within true commitment. The holes for the foxes and the nests for the birds provided secure hiding places for them to escape from their enemies, but Jesus had no place to hide. One who is committed to Jesus will have to face danger and persecution as Jesus did. The people in Jesus' hometown tried to kill Him (Luke 4:29); He was not safe in Judea (John 5:18), in Galilee, in Gadara (Matthew 8:34), or in Samaria (Luke 9:52, 53). Jesus' opponents were always after Him.

The disciple who is committed to Jesus will not escape criticism, mockery, snubs, and outright persecution. The disciples who stand up in the crowds will get shot down by the critics. By the end of the first century, the property of the followers of Christ was confiscated, and many were persecuted and put to death by methods that surpassed even Hitler's inhumane methods. Many were dipped into tar, attached to posts, and then lit like torches to provide illumination for the sports arena. Others were wrapped up in fresh animal skins and placed in the arena where starving dogs and wild animals were let loose upon them.

Persecution of the disciples of Christ in many parts of the world today does not come in such violent forms. We are more familiar with the subtle persecution of our egos. A Christian may lose his job if he does not go along with dishonest ethics. We may acquire the name of "Holy Joe" if we don't go along with the dirty jokes and innuendos. We may be called "chicken" if we don't experiment with drugs or sex.

Not only did Jesus want potential disciples to understand the commitment He wanted of them; He wanted them to come with Him with no reservations. One person who had received Jesus' invitation to follow Him had some reasons that he could not leave instantly—"Permit me first to go and bury my father" (Luke 9:59). Jesus had given the order to depart, but this man wanted to wait awhile. His life was too crowded with other responsibilities to be free to go with Jesus. He could not let go of the "worries of the world."

Looking at the situation through our eyes today, the request of this man does not seem unreasonable at all. Why couldn't Jesus wait for a funeral? The custom then was to bury a person on the same day he died; so why couldn't Jesus wait a few hours?

The funeral was not the issue. Jesus had stopped in His busy schedule for a funeral before (Luke 7:11-17); He was never too hurried to express His compassion. But this man was asking for an indefinite period of staying behind, not just for a few hours. It was the responsibility of the son to remain at home until after the father died.

This man was telling Jesus that he wanted to take care of his family and social obligations before He followed Jesus. He was, in effect, telling Jesus to wait until he could accomplish everything he had planned to do. Then if he had any time or energy left over, he could invest it in Jesus' cause. "Maybe someday I'll follow you, Jesus." He had decided to follow Jesus on His own terms. He misunderstood who was supposed to write the contract.

Jesus answered this man with a challenge that emphasized the responsibilities of discipleship: "Allow the dead to bury their own dead, but as for you, go and proclaim everywhere the kingdom of God" (Luke 9:60, NASB). Jesus was saying that there are some responsibilities that the spiritually dead can carry out. If every Christian spent all his time and energy looking after the responsibilities that anyone can do, the vital services that only a disciple of Jesus can do would be neglected.

Jesus was not suggesting that we not be involved in

any social or community or family activities, but we are not to be involved in them *only*. Christians are to be the light and salt in their communities, and responsible for their families, but they must strike a balance. Jesus knew this man. Evidently he had the tendency to procrastinate. He needed to hear Jesus' words of urgency.

Another man answered Jesus' invitation with a similar reluctance: "I will follow You, Lord; but first permit me to say good-bye to those at home" (Luke 9:61, NASB). Jesus knew what would happen if this particular man returned home. He was probably part of a strict Jewish family that would not accept Jesus as the Messiah. Jesus knew that the family would not give its consent for this man to follow an itinerant preacher. Every Jewish boy was expected to learn a profitable trade or go into the family business. Jesus sensed that this young man was too tied to his family to be able to make a firm commitment to Him.

Jesus responded in this way, "No one, after putting his hand to the plow and looking back, is fit for the kingdom of God" (9:62, NASB). Any farmer knows that plowing a straight furrow requires selecting a spot ahead at the end of the field, aiming toward it, and plowing. To look around or backwards would produce crooked furrows. It is the same situation in the realm of discipleship. We must select the proper goal and work toward it, not allowing things of the world to distract us.

We must not be rash or too reserved in our commitment to Jesus. We must be willing to lose our lives for Him. Our hearts and heads must be aiming toward the same goal, and we must be ready to bear the crosses as well as reap the blessings. That is what is involved in discipleship. Are you ready?

# CHAPTER FOUR

# A STUDY OF THE TWELVE: PETER

Why did Jesus choose men who were so different from each other to be His disciples? Was He expecting to have a continual fight on His hands? No, He wanted men who could complement each other. What one man lacked, another supplied.

Jesus intended to build His church (Matthew 16:18) with these men being the foundational pillars of that church (Ephesians 2:20; Galatians 2:9). Our physical bodies have a head and many different members with different functions, and the church is similarly designed (Ephesians 1:23; Romans 12:4-8; 1 Corinthians 12:12-26). The church has many functions (Romans 12:4) so that there will be "no division in the body, but that its parts should have equal concern for each other" (1 Corinthians 12:25).

Such a design might sound difficult. Wouldn't it seem logical that divisions would be caused by so many differences? No, on the contrary. Trouble would come with a capital "T" if we were all the same. We would be in constant competition with each other. We would all be trying to play "king on the hill," pushing our brothers and sisters aside so we could be in a more privileged position.

In my physical body, my big toe is not trying to

perform the function of my heart. My heart is not trying to usurp the position of my eyes. They are different and perform different functions, but in that diversity there is a unity. The same unity is to happen in the body of Christ. Each member lives to help other members, filling in where they lack. In that way each member is able to make his unique contribution while the fellowship and sharing that strengthens each Christian is also possible.

As we consider the lives of Jesus' twelve disciples, we can see the unity amid diversity principle manifested vividly (list of names in Mark 3:16-19). Although they were all from Galilee (Acts 1:11; 2:7), they were not alike in background and temperament. At least four of them were fishermen—Andrew, Peter, James, and John (Matthew 4:18-22). One was a political revolutionary—Simon, the Zealot. Another was a political bureaucrat when Jesus chose him—Matthew. One evidently had a background in finances since he was chosen to be the treasurer of the group, while another seemed to be somewhat overcome by financial considerations—Philip (John 6:7). One was quick to jump to conclusions—Peter, while another was slower to make decisions—Thomas. One seemed to be more socially liberal than the others, for he brought non-Jews to Jesus—Philip. Two of the disciples had terrible tempers, and Jesus nicknamed them "Sons of Thunder" (Mark 3:17). Some were up-front, public-type leaders while others were so much in the background that we know little about them.

Jesus did not select these men because they were perfect specimens of humanity, or spiritual giants. They were immature; they needed to change. They learned to grow under Jesus' leadership.

38

Jesus did not see perfection, but He did see potential in them. And as we seek to make disciples, we should also look for the potential in people. We must look beyond what a person is to see what He can become. No person should be cemented into his present character and conduct. We should look for "moldability." Is that person open to change? Is he teachable and pliable?

For a person to be willing to become a disciple is to be willing to become different—different from what he has been and is presently. Changing is exciting, but it also can be threatening and painful. It is certainly costly, for a person must deny himself so he can become like Christ. To be unwilling to change is to say we have already arrived. A person does not begin the role of discipleship with the idea, "I'm O.K., you're O.K., Jesus." We are in no way able to place ourselves *alongside* Jesus as equals. Instead we are to feel, "You're O.K., Jesus, but I'm not; so I repent." Then we are able to walk *behind* Jesus and follow His example. Only in that way will we be able to change into Jesus' likeness.

Now, let us look at Jesus' twelve disciples and discover what walking behind Jesus is all about.

## PETER

*The Rock.* Peter could have been the "Diotrephes" of the group of disciples. Diotrephes was a dictator in his congregation who thought that he and only he was right on every issue (3 John 9-10). Every board meeting would have to go his way, or it would not go any way. If the board were discussing a financial matter, the Diotrephes-type person would think that he knew more than the bank president. If the board were discussing a building project, the Diotrephes-type person would think he knew more than the elder who is a building contractor. Peter had this type of disposition.

The first time Jesus met Simon, He gave him a name that matched his personality: "You are Simon son of John. You will be called Cephas" (John 1:42). Cephas meant Peter or "little rock." Jesus was saying, "Simon, you are so hard-headed, I'm going to name you 'the rock.'"

God can use the "rock" kind of people. It is good to be firm when you are taking a stand on the truth. God needs more people like that, for they are not led around by various philosophies or ideas as puppies on a leash. But these people must be careful not to be so stuck on themselves that will not bend. They must not be so firm that they cannot be changed. Too much firmness does not make a true disciple, for a disciple must be a learner and a follower. A disciple cannot always be trying to be the one who is in charge. Jesus will not share the Lordship with any human.

We have hope because few people are "harder" than Peter was when Jesus met him. We can learn from Peter that underneath the shell of hardness is a soft spot. Although Peter's mind was like concrete, it had not completely settled. Jesus could still make an impression on him and mold him. It took time and patience, but to Jesus Peter was worth it.

*Insensitivity.* The "rock" kind of people often lack sensitivity to other people's feelings and needs. That lack is further heightened when a person's job requires that he relate to things rather than people. That was Peter's situation. He spent most of his time with things like the boats, the rigging, and the fish. So as soon as possible, Jesus exposed Peter to the compassion side of leadership.

When Jesus entered Peter's house, he was not so busy teaching truths that he did not have the time to give personal attention to Peter's mother-in-law. She was very sick; so Jesus healed her. Later that same day Jesus took the time to heal many people who were gathered there (Mark 1:29-34). Jesus showed Peter that He was not only full of truth; He was also full of caring.

Jesus taught with authority and acted with authority (Mark 1:21-27). Peter could identify with that aspect of Jesus because that is the way he liked to act. He wanted to speak with authority and have others do as he said. But as he observed Jesus, he learned that authoritativeness must be balanced with caring and compassion for the needs and problems of others.

Peter's actions on the Day of Pentecost reflect this balance that he had learned from Jesus. He stood up and spoke with authority (Acts 2:14-41) and immediately followed that with compassion for people's needs (Acts 2:44-47). Very soon after Pentecost, Peter's compassion extended to a crippled man at the gate of the temple (Acts 3:1-10).

Peter, the disciple, had listened carefully to Jesus' teachings. He remembered the parable Jesus told about the men who were on the way to the temple but had no time to help the man who had been beaten and robbed and left for dead on the side of the road. Now he was on his way to the temple, and here was a man in need. Peter decided to follow the example of the caring Samaritan rather than the hard-nosed priest and Levite of Jesus' parable. Peter did what every disciple must do—listen and learn; then live it out.

This type of teaching-discipleship experience needs to be repeated in every church today. Every congregation should be a discipling workshop. We get many young men coming to Bible college who think the total job of the preacher is to preach. Why? Because they have not been properly exposed to any other aspect of the preacher's life. The first place to teach what it means to be a minister of a church is not at the Bible college but in the church. Every person who leads should do what Jesus did with Peter. He should expose some of his students to experiences that balance leading/teaching with caring for others' needs. How? By taking the students with him to minister to the lonely, the grieving, the sick, and the poor. We could develop a whole church of "Good Samaritans" that way. Being good and kind comes naturally to some, but others need to catch the attitude as Peter did from observing compassion in action.

*Independence.* The "rock" kind of person can easily forget that he needs help himself. It is tempting for him to feel he is a self-made person and is independent of everyone else. Peter had an important lesson to learn in this area.

The morning after Jesus healed so many people, Peter woke up and found that his house guest was gone. Jesus had gone, but Peter did not know where or why. Peter went looking for Him and found Him in a solitary place praying (Mark 1:35-37). Peter learned that no one, regardless of how much authority he has, should think that he needs no help. Everyone needs help at times. Jesus was humble enough to pray and ask for God's guidance, even though He was God in the flesh.

It is easy for leaders today to teach their followers

that they are doing so much for the Lord simply because of the personal effort they put out. Consequently, we are discipling people who become work-a-holics. We must allow the students to realize that much prayer is needed in God's service; it is not just energy and effort that makes success.

Seeing Jesus pray made an impression on Peter. Before he spoke on the Day of Pentecost, he prayed with the others who were gathered (Acts 1:10-14). The early church continued in prayer (Acts 2:42). After Peter and John were released from the authorities that had arrested them, they met with God's people—to pray (Acts 4:23-31). Peter had learned the importance of prayer in the life of a disciple of Jesus.

*Uncontrolled Tongue.* At times in Peter's life it seemed as if the primary purpose for his mouth was as a depository for both his feet. He put his mouth into high gear while his mind was still in neutral. He was often an arrogant, bragging, impulsive, boisterous know-it-all. He told Jesus He was wrong (Mark 8:31, 32); he criticized Jesus for asking a certain question (Luke 8:43-45); he wanted to put Elijah and Moses on an equal level with Jesus even after he had declared Jesus to be the Messiah (Matthew 17:4); he thoughtlessly declared that "even if all fall away on account of you, . . . I will never disown you" (Matthew 26:33-35).

But Jesus lovingly taught him self-control. Peter heard Jesus admit that even *He* did not know everything (Matthew 24:36); he observed as Jesus controlled His own speech by not paying back verbal jabs for the verbal jabs He had received. Peter noticed those times when Jesus' words built people up instead of tearing them down.

Jesus also directly and pointedly disciplined Peter. On one occasion Peter received a very sharp rebuke: "Out of my sight, Satan! You are a stumbling block to Me; you do not have in mind the things of God, but the things of men" (Matthew 16:23). That rebuke immediately detoured the irresponsible way Peter was using his mouth in that situation.

Discipling people involves disciplining them. We do not help the kingdom of God by letting people continue to damage themselves and others with their tongues. We are told to use our tongues "for building others up according to their needs, that it may benefit those who listen" (Ephesians 4:29). We are told that "if you keep on biting and devouring each other, watch out or you will be destroyed by each other" (Galatians 5:15).

We can help others control their tongues by being good examples in how we use our tongues in their presence. Do our disciples hear us make rash promises which we never intend to keep? What do they hear us say when we are criticized or questioned? Do we often speak with "chips on our shoulders"?

Research in communication reveals that effective communication rests upon three things—what is said, the tone of voice, and the nonverbal communication. Which of these is most important? Most people would say the content of our talk is the most important. But *what* we say accounts for only seven percent of effective communication. The tone of voice accounts for thirty-eight percent. (I can say one thing in a certain tone of voice to my children and nothing happens. I can say the same thing to my children in another tone and they move!) The words "I love you" said in a mean tone of voice take on a whole different connotation. However, nonverbal communication accounts for fifty-five percent of effective communication. The raised eyebrow, the smile, the nodding of the head, a tear—all these mean so much in communicating.

One time all it took was a look from Jesus to remind Peter that his impulsive mouth had been troublesome again. "The Lord turned and looked straight at Peter. Then Peter remembered the word the Lord had spoken to him . . ." (Luke 22:61). In that look, Jesus reminded Peter that he had not yet reached the level of maturity that Peter had been bragging about not long before.

Peter learned how to control his tongue by following Jesus' example. Peter's reply to being arrested was well thought-out, mature, and helpful (Acts 4:8-12). Peter's refusal to obey the command to be silent was not with the rash words which would have come from him in his immature days. He did not say, "I won't obey you, and you can't make me." Instead he caused his accusers to put themselves in his place; he caused them to think. "Judge for yourselves whether it is right in God's sight to obey you rather than God" (Acts 4:19).

When a dispute arose in the church, Peter did not stand up and do all the talking. He listened and did not say a word until there had been much discussion (Acts 15:7ff). Peter had changed; Peter had matured. He had learned from Jesus about the beauty and benefit of thought-out communication.

Probably more damage has been done in the church by the misuse of the tongue than by the misunderstanding of the truth. There is no such thing as a disciped person who is not trying to control his tongue. James wrote that if we can control our tongues, then we can control the whole self (James 3:1-12).

*Unforgiving.* Peter's "rock" kind of personality also made it easy for him to hold a grudge. Once he asked Jesus, "Lord, how many times shall I forgive my brother when he sins against me?" Then he suggested the answer that he thought Jesus should give, "Up to seven times?" (Matthew 18:21). I cannot help but think that Peter had a particular person in mind who had offended him seven times. Peter had had enough. The "rock" was wanting to fall on someone. But Jesus' answer fell upon Peter and shattered his possible plans for revenge, "I tell you, not seven times, but seventy-seven times." Jesus was saying, "Peter, quit keeping score."

Peter's tendency to keep score was apparent in the Garden of Gethsemane on the night Jesus was betrayed. Peter drew a sword and cut off the right ear of one of those who had come to arrest Jesus (John 18:10). Peter was angry and violent; he still had some learning to do. In the following hours, Peter learned how Jesus handled opposition. Jesus refused to call down angels to defend himself. Peter observed how Jesus didn't even use His tongue to defend himself. Jesus remained silent through most of His trial, and He did not even hint that He was angry. When Jesus was hurting on the cross, it would have seemed quite natural for His words to be vindictive. Instead, He spoke with compassion and forgiveness. "Father, forgive them, for they do not know what they are doing" (Luke 23:34).

As a learning disciple of Jesus, Peter became forgiving. In his sermon in Acts 2, he made clear that the people had murdered Jesus, but he also made clear that they could be forgiven (2:23, 38). Then he fellow-shipped with those who were responsible for Jesus' death (2:42). Many years later, he extended the right hand of fellowship to Paul, whose one purpose in life had been to exterminate Christians (Galatians 1:18; 2:7-10).

Peter learned to forgive and not fight back. He replaced the sword of steel with the sword of the Spirit. But what about us? Are we forgiving one another? Are we peacemakers or peacebreakers? Have you ever noticed that some churches go from one fight to another? Why? Because they have been used to bearing grudges, being unforgiving, and becoming angry. Such a church cannot make any significant contribution to God's cause unless the cycle is broken. We must not associate with those who are always "hot under the collar" (Proverbs 22:24, 25), for we will learn their ways. God commands that we not allow a factious person to spread his cancer throughout the body of Christ (Titus 3:10; Romans 16:17; Proverbs 22:10).

*Prejudiced.* As a Jew, Peter had been reared as a segregationist—believing that the Gentiles were always to remain separate from the Jews. It took Peter a long time to grow out of this belief. Some aspects of character take longer to mature than others.

Jesus led His disciples through Gentile Samaria (John 4); He healed a Greek woman's daughter (Mark 7:24-30). Jesus told many parables that taught that the Gentiles would also inherit the kingdom (Matthew 21, 22). And Peter heard Jesus give the Great Commission to go and make disciples of all the nations (Matthew 28:19). Jesus was telling His disciples to disciple people from all nationalities; it was not just that they were to go into different geographical areas. Peter quoted Old Testament Scriptures in his sermon on Pentecost that made it clear that any ethnic group was a part of God's plan of salvation (Acts 2:17, 21); so he understood the truth in theory. But prejudices take a long time to overcome. And God gave Peter the time.

Ten years after that sermon on Pentecost, Peter had still not entered a Gentile's house (Acts 10:28). It took a special vision from God to get him to do so. The vision included all sorts of animals. God told him to kill and eat them (Acts 10:10-13). When Peter saw the food as ethnically related, he thought about the people connected with that food. Just as we think about a certain people when we hear "chop suey" or "pizza," he thought of the Gentiles when he saw pork. To eat that food would mean Peter could associate with those people, even eat with them! Peter again challenged the teaching of his Master: "By no means, Lord" (10:14, NASB). But the Lord was patient and kept prodding Peter so he would understand. Peter finally realized that God was telling him that he should associate with Gentiles (10:28, 34, 35).

After the vision, when he fully understood God's wishes, Peter proceeded to evangelize Gentiles and to even stay in their homes. He learned to eat at their tables and sleep in their beds. He had learned that God is no segregationist and began to apply it in his own life.

Peter was criticized for this action (11:1-3), but he did not back down (11:4-17). Even at that, Peter went back and forth on this racial issue. While in Antioch, he ate with Gentiles as long as there weren't any Jews around to know about it. When Jews appeared, he turned away from the Gentiles. Integration is toughest when the segregationists are looking (Galatians 2:11-13).

But Peter matured gradually. Evidently he took Paul's rebuke of his actions in a good spirit (Galatians 2:13-21), for later, when writing to Christians scattered throughout the world (1 Peter 1:1), he said those who "once were not a people" (Gentiles) had become "the people of God" (2:10).

I imagine that many church members are as determined about the racial issue as Peter was. It is extremely difficult to overcome prejudice, but God certainly considers this an area of needed growth. He wants His disciples on earth to live with each other the way we will live together in Heaven.

Who are we to mock God's creation? Who are we to suggest that some people He created are inferior and others are superior? God will not send us a vision as He did to Peter. Instead He shares with us the written revelation of that vision and expects us to learn from it.

God was patient with Peter's prejudices, and Peter was willing to change when he saw clearly that his stance was not God's. We may be every bit as prejudiced as Peter was, but are we as open to change as he was? It was not easy for Peter to sit down and eat with a person of another race. He was uncomfortable and his stomach was queasy. But he was willing to grow in every aspect toward Jesus, his leader.

Are we as patient with those we are teaching as God was with Peter? It took him over ten years to overcome his prejudices. A part of disciple-making is giving people time to grow out of some of the hang-ups in their lives.

*Courage.* Peter was an interesting mixture of cow-

49

ardice and courage. He was courageous when he was with his peers. He could tell them exactly what he would and would not do. But at one time in his life he became a marshmallow when faced with his enemies (Luke 22:56-60). He learned from Jesus how to have courage in the difficult times. Without a word Jesus took the beatings from the soldiers. He lay on the cross of his own accord without having to be tied to it. Jesus declared, "I lay down my life for the sheep" (John 10:15), and He voluntarily gave up His life.

That must have made an impression on Peter, for within two months he manifested that same kind of courage. He refused to be intimidated by the highest court in the land (Acts 3). When beaten, he immediately resumed the activities that caused him to be beaten (Acts 5:40, 42).

Tradition says Peter was martyred for his faith in Jesus. When it came time to attach him to the cross, he requested to be crucified upside down because he was not worthy to die in the same manner as the Lord. He had come a long way from his immature, arrogant spirit. Peter was willing to change. Thus he was able to learn the true meaning of discipleship at the feet of the greatest teacher ever known—Jesus.

Are you ready for such discipleship? Are you as willing to change as Peter was?

# CHAPTER FIVE

# A STUDY OF THE TWELVE: THE "OBSCURE" DISCIPLES

## ANDREW

Andrew was a man who was secure in his business but did not want to be restricted by that responsibility while so much was going wrong in his land. When he heard that John the Baptist was leading a national revival and speaking about the coming of the Messiah, he left his fishing business and became John's disciple. That was a courageous thing for a family man to do (the disciples were married and traveled with their wives, 1 Corinthians 9:5—remember Peter had a mother-in-law, Mark 1:30).

Andrew cared more about souls than about fish in the sea and probably helped baptize many people who had come to turn from their old lives to the new. But Andrew was not cemented to John the Baptist. As soon as John pointed out the Messiah, Andrew followed Jesus (John 1:37, 40). It is tempting to hear a great speaker and then allow him to become an idol, but Andrew was not so inclined. He had a keen sense of spiritual discernment. He had anticipated becoming a disciple of the Messiah (about whom John the Baptist spoke) even before he had met Jesus. Jesus did not have to look a certain way or have a certain type of personality. The fact that He was the Messiah was enough for Andrew. When that fact was clear, Andrew followed Jesus.

Andrew was the only disciple who we know had made up his mind in this way to follow Jesus when He appeared. It is possible that there are many today who would be disciples of Jesus if they only knew He was the spiritual leader they have been looking for. Perhaps they are simply waiting to be introduced to the Savior as Andrew was. If it is true (and I believe it is) that we were made in the image of God and are restless until we are reunited with Him, then I suspect that most of the religions of the world are attempts to make the reuniting possible. Many of those in these religions may just be waiting to be introduced to Jesus.

Andrew was a committed disciple. He was not only willing to leave his business and to follow Jesus immediately after his introduction to Him, but he was also ready to introduce others to Jesus. Andrew wasted no time in finding his brother, Simon, and bringing him to meet Jesus (John 1:41, 42).

Andrew was the first apostle to spend any time with Jesus (John 1:38, 39). He was among the four disciples who accompanied Jesus to a marriage feast where Jesus did His first miracle (John 2:1-11). Only he and the other three (Peter, Philip, and Nathanael) traveled with Jesus to Jerusalem for the Passover feast and saw Him cleanse the temple (John 2:12-22). They remained with Jesus and began baptizing more people than even John the Baptist (John 4:1, 2). On the way back to Galilee, they saw Jesus minister to a Samaritan woman (John 4). While in Galilee, Jesus evidently gave the four a "mini-vacation," because some time later He came to the lake and called them from their boats to follow Him (Matthew 4:18).

What did these experiences teach Andrew? He learned that Jesus cared about people. Jesus was not too busy to attend a wedding and to help out when needed. Jesus attended a religious feast, but at the same time He felt strongly about the need to enable the people to pray in the proper atmosphere; thus he cleansed the temple. The manufactured inflation of prices just for the occasion was not God's way of promoting worship. Jesus also broke through Jewish tradition by talking with a Samaritan woman and was even willing to drink from her cup.

Andrew's own contribution was done mostly behind the scenes. In a crowd of thousands of people, Andrew would spend time looking for the lonely. He noted the compassion of Jesus and began to apply it in his own life. Who would notice a small boy sitting amongst a large crowd? Andrew did.

In a crowd of five thousand men plus women and children (probably between 10,000 and 12,000 people), Andrew moved among them. He got to know the people individually by listening and talking to them and showing that he cared. When the food ran out and there was not enough money to buy food for so many, Andrew knew of a little boy in the crowd—knew him so well that he knew the contents of his lunch bag! And not only that, Andrew knew exactly where that boy could be found in the huge masses of people (John 6:8-9). Andrew cared enough about people to remember them.

Everytime we notice Andrew, he is bringing some-one to Jesus. He was so apt to introduce others to Jesus that the other apostles went to him when they knew of people who wanted to meet Jesus (John 12:22).

Probably the most significant contribution of An-drew was his willingness to introduce his brother to Jesus. He knew that Peter would almost immediately overshadow him (Andrew); that was Peter's way. An-drew had probably been in the sidelines all his life because of Peter. For once, Andrew could have been involved in something without Peter's presence and his take-charge attitude. It would have been tempting for Andrew to bypass Peter and be the only family member to be a part of Jesus' group of disciples.

But Andrew had been a disciple of John the Baptist and had learned from John's example of humility. John loved to point people to Jesus, knowing that Jesus was going to outshine John's efforts and popu-larity. John did not mind. He said, "He must become greater; I must become less" (John 3:30).

Andrew knew of Peter's natural leadership abilities underneath his rough and hard exterior, and pur-posely introduced him to Jesus. He knew what Jesus could do for Peter, and we have no hint that Andrew ever resented the "Peter-come-lately" emerging as the leader of the group and being promised the keys to the kingdom by Jesus (Matthew 16:19).

As each one of us is striving to become a disciple of Jesus, are we doing as Andrew did? Or are we so attached to our businesses that we are not free to follow Jesus as we should? We may not have to walk away from our businesses to follow Jesus as Andrew did, but we must be willing to do so if the need arises.

What are our priorities? Do we consider our work, our hobbies, our club and community activities more important than our service for Jesus?

Are we as ready to introduce others to Jesus as Andrew was? Jesus did not give us an impossible task when He told us to go ' ' ? world and evangelize. Even today, with population e ﹐ ﹐nding so rapidly, the task is not impossible. If each Christian witnessed to just one person a year, and that new Christian witnessed to one other, and the chain continued, the entire population of the world could be reached for Jesus in thirty-three years.

Andrew's experiences with Jesus included wedding feasts and worship services. Are we helping people to understand the broad diversification of what God's influence could be in the world, or are we giving people the idea that being locked up in a room with books to study is the way for a spiritual mountaintop experience?

Do we notice the insignificant people in the crowds as Andrew reached out to the small lad with the lunch? Andrew's observation of Jesus' attitude with children must have impressed him and made him realize the importance of all people—young or old, rich or poor. We should be impressed with Jesus' attitude with people and treat everyone as a person of value, no matter what his station in life, how he dresses, or where he is from.

Are we willing to allow others to overshadow and outshine us without feelings of resentment as Andrew was? One of the most disappointing things I see across the country in our churches is the way some "senior" ministers suppress their associate ministers. The senior ministers should be committed to developing their associate ministers to become great servants of God, allowing them to preach, counsel, perform weddings and funerals, preside at the worship services, attend conventions, and the like. We must be willing to spot people with Peter's potential and not be threatened when they advance above and beyond us. After all, we are to be concerned about advancing God's kingdom—not our status in the kingdom.

According to some historians Andrew eventually evangelized in southern Russia. There he was scourged and crucified, being tied, not nailed, to the cross so that he would suffer longer. He encouraged the Christians and prayed, and he regarded the cross as his ultimate opportunity to honor the Lord. He hung on the cross for two days.

Yes, discipleship is demanding—both in being a disciple and in developing disciples.

## PHILIP

Philip was from the same town as Andrew and Peter and probably knew them well (John 1:44). But Jesus found Philip and issued the call, "Follow me" (1:43). Philip had probably heard about Jesus and knew whom he was following.

Philip was an active follower, not a passive one. He immediately found another to bring to Jesus. He told Nathanael: "We have found the one Moses wrote about in the Law, and about whom the prophets also wrote—Jesus of Nazareth, the son of Joseph" (1:45). Philip was not argumentative as Peter was. He did not argue when Nathanael raised an objection: "Nazareth! Can anything good come from there?" He simply replied, "Come and see" (1:46).

Philip did not walk away when Nathanael expressed

his critical view, nor did he send him away, saying, "Okay, you've made your bed, now lie in it." He did not become discouraged by Nathanel's seeming lack of interest; instead he said, "Spend some time with me and observe." Philip did not give up but kept issuing the invitation to come. He was being a friend to Nathanael and hoping to bring him to Jesus by that association.

How many of us follow Philip's example when we are seeking to disciple others? Do we argue or become too easily discouraged? Do we act as friends seeking to do others a favor, or would we rather do our discipling by remote control—invite others to church and then see them no more? It is interesting that many of these disciples were anxious to bring others to Jesus and did so at the very beginning of their discipleship, while many today still have not brought anyone to Christ.

Philip seems to have been an analytical person. On one occasion, Jesus asked him, "Where shall we buy bread for these people to eat?" (John 6:5). Philip looked at the crowd and calculated quickly: "Eight months' wages would not buy enough bread for each one to have a bite" (6:7). At another time, Philip made a request of Jesus, showing this same characteristic: "Lord, show us the Father and that will be enough for us" (John 14:8).

Jesus did not criticize Philip for thinking things out. He asked Philip questions and allowed Philip the same privilege. But He did not allow Philip's analysis to be the last word. On both occasions Philip had to be corrected in his thinking; but Jesus did not squelch him. He enabled Philip's mind to be stretched.

Do we do that with the disciples we are making?

Or do we squelch their ideas and put them down as if they had no brains? A person with a good mind should not think that he has to put his intellect aside to serve Jesus. He must be encouraged to search out truth in all its aspects, and illuminate the truth for others. We must remember that all types of people can fellowship together and can serve Jesus—even the arrogant and the analytical (like Peter and Philip). And all kinds of people can be molded into Christlikeness.

Historians record for us that Philip went to Scythia and preached there twenty years. He went to Hierapolis after that and evangelized and ministered to people who worshiped the god Mars, a serpent-dragon god. Philip was killed by being pierced through the thighs and hung upside down. He used his mind to serve Jesus and took his discipleship seriously. Do we?

### NATHANAEL

Nathanael (Bartholomew) was skeptical when he first heard about Jesus (John 1:46), but he did not allow his first reaction to restrict his thinking. He was open enough to let the future facts and experiences guide him. Jesus said about him, "Here is a true Israelite, in whom there is nothing false" (1:47). Jesus was saying that Nathanael was not putting up a false front but was being sincere in his skepticism.

A person can become a disciple even though he may at first be skeptical, as long as that skepticism is real and not a screen to hide behind. It is possible to make skeptical comments in order to keep oneself from making a real commitment to follow Jesus.

Nathanael was under a fig tree when Jesus first saw him (John 1:48). Fig trees were often shelters under which rabbis studied. It is possible that Nathanael had been studying the Scriptures or praying when Jesus saw him. If so, it is no wonder that Jesus called him a *true* Israelite (1:47). Nathanael was not just religious on the outside but also on the inside.

Nathanael proves to us that a person with doubts can come to a faith in Jesus. But we cannot argue or belittle the doubts away. Intellectualizing is not what Nathanael needed; he needed to experience Jesus— to see and hear Jesus in action. No one can draw people to Jesus any better than Jesus himself. So we must let others see Jesus through our words and our lives.

According to history, Nathanael preached in India and Phrygia. There are two different accounts about his death. One account says he was put into a sack and thrown into the sea while the other says he was beaten and crucified. Whatever happened, his death points out again the cost of discipleship.

## OTHER "OBSCURE" DISCIPLES

We have no Biblical knowledge about *James*, the son of Alphaeus, *Thaddaeus* (also called Judas), and *Simon* the Zealot. Their names appear with the others in the listings of the twelve in Matthew 10:3, 4; Mark 3:18; Luke 6:15, 16; and Acts 1:13. Even though the Biblical record about these men leaves them in relative obscurity, we can learn from them.

The gospel record (Matthew, Mark, Luke, and John) was not written to give us a detailed report about the twelve disciples, but to tell us about Jesus. And although the book of Acts has the "apostles" in its title, the book is not about them. Only four of the original twelve were included in the book of Acts (except for the listing of all of them). Two of the four were mentioned only in order to record their deaths (Judas Iscariot and James). John is mentioned only briefly (Acts 3-5). Of the twelve, Peter gets the most mention, but the book is certainly not about him. Acts is simply telling what God continued to do through His church in expanding Christianity to all kinds of people.

Yet the twelve disciples do not seem upset that no inspired writing expands upon their individual lives, and that in itself should tell us something about discipleship. True disciples are not concerned about how much they themselves are being spotlighted; their concern is that Jesus gets spotlighted. It has been said, "The world has yet to see what God can do with a person who does not care who gets the credit." But we *have* seen what God can do with such people. These "obscure" disciples were dynamic leaders that caused Christianity to spread over the whole populated world at that time (as history records).

These men were selected to be in Jesus' special group after an all-night prayer meeting (Luke 6:12). Jesus selected them to be with Him, to experience with Him, and to learn from Him. They could be looked upon as interns of Jesus or His students in a traveling Bible college.

Jesus sent them out two by two to preach and to perform miracles (Matthew 10:2-8). They learned by that experience not to worry about their provisions (10:9, 10). They learned that they were to depend upon others and not seek to be put on a pedestal above others (10:11, 12). They learned that their message would receive violent opposition from the very people who should be glad to receive it (10:16-18). They learned that God would give them the words to say (10:19, 20). They learned that they were to become like Jesus (10:24, 25). They learned that they were to share all that Jesus had taught them (10:27) and not to fear those who could kill only the body. Instead they were to fear Him who could destroy the soul (10:28). They learned that God was concerned about the smallest details in their lives (10:29, 30). They learned that their message would divide people; so they shouldn't preach just to maintain peace and harmony (10:21, 34-37). They learned that being a disciple meant being willing to bear a cross (10:38, 39), being willing to die for their teacher. Yes, Jesus' disciples learned a great deal, and in later life they applied what they had learned quite adequately.

After Jesus arose from the dead, He told them to go to Jerusalem and wait. But wait a minute! Wouldn't that be dangerous? That is the city that crucified Jesus and knew that these men were His disciples. The disciples of a teacher were to receive whatever their teacher received. Jesus was arrested and crucified! Were the disciples also to share that? It is no wonder that they fled when Jesus was put on trial. But things had changed. After three days, Jesus arose. So now their fears were gone, and they could go without hesitation to Jerusalem and wait.

By telling them to wait, Jesus was saying, "Don't act impulsively. Don't try to run ahead of me. First, get equipped for the task ahead." That is the same message we need to receive today. We must learn to wait on God. It is tough, but it is a part of discipleship. Moses was to be used by God, but God waited eighty years before using him. Joseph knew from his dreams that God would use him in a great way, but he had to wait years in a dungeon before it came to pass. Waiting is hard, but it pays off.

Later we read of the disciples' remaining in Jerusalem in the midst of much persecution (Acts 8:1). That took courage, but by this time these men were unshakeable. They were applying well what they had learned from their experiences resulting from their being sent out by Jesus (Matthew 10).

Other histories tell us what these "obscure" disciples did and how they died. Thaddaeus preached in Syria, Arabia, Mesopotamia, and Persia. He suffered martyrdom in Syria. James, the son of Alphaeus, preached in Syria and was stoned to death by the Jews. Simon the Zealot traveled and preached in Egypt, Cyrene, Africa, Libya, Mesopotamia, Persia, and Britain—where he was crucified.

## SUMMARY

We can learn much about discipleship from these men. We can learn that we do not become disciples to become popular. We become disciples to serve, not to be noticed. Much of our work may never be noticed until Jesus returns. What we do does not have to be reported in the church paper or mentioned from the pulpit. When we feel slighted or think about quitting because no one notices all the work we do for God, we should remember these obscure disciples of Jesus.

We can learn that we must not be in too big a hurry to get things done or try to run ahead of God's plans. We need to balance all our activity with waiting at times. We need patience as well as productivity.

We can also recognize that discipleship is not a bed of roses. Disciples of Jesus will be opposed, neglected, and rejected. We can know that God will provide our needs, but we must realize that those provisions do not mean that we will not get hurt. We can know, however, that no matter what happens to us socially or physically because of our commitment to Christ, we have the promise of eternal joy and healing in Heaven. And just as the disciples stuck with their commitment to Jesus when the going got rough, so should we. The disciples stayed in Jerusalem when the opposition was the sharpest, and they were used by God to bring Christianity to those who had been very much against it.

Are you willing to be an "obscure" disciple? Are you willing to work behind the scenes while others get the spotlight? Specifically what do you do? Are you truly anxious to introduce others to Jesus? Do you persevere even when people are critical? Do you help others work through their doubts instead of shutting them out? Are you patient to wait on God's direction, and do you "stick with it" when the going gets rough?

# CHAPTER SIX

# A STUDY OF THE TWELVE: JAMES AND JOHN

Although James and John were not twins, by the way they were described in the Scripture, we might almost get the idea that they were identical in many ways. Until the final week in Jesus' life, every time one is mentioned, the other is also. They certainly practiced togetherness.

Jesus called them to discipleship early in His ministry. They were fishermen, and they seem to have been wealthy. When Jesus called them to follow Him, they did not only leave their father in the boat but also the "hired men" (Mark 1:20). Their mother, Salome, traveled with Jesus' group and helped support His ministry financially (Matthew 27:55, 56; Mark 15:40, 41).

## THEIR TEMPERS

James and John must have been spoiled as boys growing up. Not long after Jesus called them, He nicknamed them "Sons of Thunder" (Mark 3:17), for they sounded off like thunder when things did not go their way. They must have been throwing tantrums to get their way ever since they were young.

But Jesus taught James and John that an uncontrollable temper is not useful in the work of the kingdom. On one occasion Jesus and His disciples were traveling through Samaria. As far as the Jews were concerned, Samaria was the biracial ghetto of the world. At one time the area was occupied by true-blue Jews, but after the Assyrians captured the ten tribes who dwelt there, the Jews intermarried and became totally multiracial. Out of those historical experiences grew fierce racial hostilities between the Samaritans and the Jews.

Although the Samaritans worshiped the same God, used the same Scriptures (or part of them), and looked for the Messiah, they established their own temple to be competitive with the temple in Jerusalem. The Jews ranked these Samaritans with Gentiles and strangers (Matthew 10:5; John 4:9). The term *Samaritan* itself was one of reproach (John 8:48). In fact, one rabbi so despised the Samaritans that he taught that Samaria was a "no-nation." One widely used Jewish proverb stated, "A piece of bread given by a Samaritan is more unclean than swine's flesh."

The hatred between the two peoples was so intense that Jews would avoid Samaria when traveling between Judea and Galilee. Although Samaria was on the straight-line route, the Jews would detour several miles east, cross the Jordan river, and then go back west after bypassing Samaria.

But Jesus would not bypass Samaria. He used the opportunity to travel through the area to teach His disciples valuable lessons. The trip between Galilee and Jerusalem would take three days; thus the group would have to spend at least one night in Samaria. In this particular instance, Jesus evidently sent some of

His disciples ahead of the group to make arrangements for the night in an inn.

As the disciples approached the inn, they could have noticed the few donkeys parked outside and thought, "There must be plenty of room. There are only a few donkeys and the 'no vacancy' sign is not out." But the people were not about to let Jesus' group stay there, and they did not politely brush off the disciples—they rudely rejected them. The text makes clear that Jesus and the disciples were not welcome "because He was heading for Jerusalem" (Luke 9:51-53).

When the disciples came back to the group with news of the rejection, the thunderous brothers (James and John) broke out into a rage. They asked Jesus if they could call down fire from Heaven to burn up the entire village—men, women, and children—everything (Luke 9:54).

Jesus could have kicked those two men out of the group right then. Such dispositions were opposed to Jesus' way. Wouldn't they be an embarrassment to Jesus? Surely people who saw the way they acted would misunderstand Jesus' life-style. Some might say, "If that is what following Jesus means, I will not follow. I'm just as good as they are. What a bunch of hypocrites." But Jesus was not interested in men for their abilities in public relations. He was interested in discipling men, which meant teaching and encouraging them to *change* their actions and attitudes.

Jesus rebuked James and John: "You do not know what kind of spirit you are of, for the Son of Man did not come to destroy men's lives, but to save them" (Luke 9:55, 56—see the footnote in the New International Version). What was Jesus' solution to the rejection? It was simply to go to "another village" (9:56). What an important lesson Jesus taught!

Did James and John learn from that experience? They certainly did. Later, James' very life was threatened; yet there is no hint that he tried to fight back. He was the first recorded apostle to suffer execution because of his faith (Acts 12:2).

John was one of the two apostles who came to Samaria soon after the city was evangelized to give to the Samaritans the recognition of fellowship and the ability to do miracles (Acts 8:14-18). How James and John had changed! That is what discipleship demands. Doing what Jesus would do.

Are we able to disciple those with quick tempers? Are they changing because they have noticed how we don't "sweat the small stuff"? Can they accept other options (such as "going to another village") without fretting and fuming? Can they understand that "in all things God works for the good of those who love him . . ." (Romans 8:28)? Are they changing their attitudes of racial prejudice? Or are we feeding them with our own attitudes of complaining, bitterness, and quick anger?

## THEIR SELFISHNESS

James and John also had to mature beyond the "little-boy" stage in their attitudes of selfishness. On two separate occasions, their selfishness was made apparent.

Once John showed his intolerance for any "competition." A man from "another group" was casting out demons; so John reported back to Jesus and the group: "We tried to stop him, because he is not one of us" (Luke 9:49). He must have been shocked with

Jesus' reply, for Jesus made it clear that He was not sectarian and that they should broaden their understanding,'' for whoever is not against you is for you'' (9:50).

How about us? Do we selfishly narrow our group and fellowship to those in our congregation or Bible study group? Too many times we decide to join or not to join a group on the basis of whether or not the group agrees with all our opinions, traditions, or methods. Have forgotten that it is Jesus who unites us? If we are in Christ, we are in the same heavenly family regardless of our "earthly" group.

Do we ever try to block the progress of others because they are "not one of us"? Do we ever try to help them by announcing their activities, praying for them, or fellowshipping with them? Too often our churches are entities unto themselves, showing no concern for sister congregations. We deliberately plan activities on the same night as theirs or are completely silent about others' problems and programs.

The selfish attitude of James and John also raised its ugly head when they wanted to be designated as the number two and number three men in the kingdom. At least they allowed Jesus to have the number one spot!

Evidently they had been accustomed to being the superstars at home and wanted to continue in privileged slots. So they asked their mother to ask Jesus to assure their status (Matthew 20:20, 21). She had probably voiced their desires to their father many times and been successful; so why not use the same plan of manipulation with Jesus? And besides, Salome would probably have much influence with Jesus since she was providing part of His financial support (Matthew 27:55) and may have been the sister of Jesus' mother, Mary (see Matthew 27:56; John 19:25).

Jesus did not rebuke the disciples for their desire or for the question they asked. However, He did tell them they did not understand what they were asking. Since the greatest one in a group is the one who serves everyone else, they were actually asking for more serving responsibilities (Matthew 20:22, 25-27). They could indeed become great if they drank of the cup of death that Jesus would soon drink (Matthew 20:22). But could they do that?

Jesus not only answered their request with words; He also answered them with the example of His life. Jesus was not only a master and a teacher; He was also a servant of mankind. He entered His ministry witht the commitment to serve (Luke 4:18, 19), and He never wavered from that commitment. He summarized His ministry by saying, "The Son of Man did not come to be served, but to serve, and to give his life as a ransom for many" (Matthew 20:28).

It is so easy for Christians to get the gleam of being superstars in their eyes. We live in a world that greatly rewards the performers. Many work for Jesus just to hear the applause or to climb the status ladder. It is not wrong for people to recognize good work and praise it, but it is wrong for God's servants to work for that praise. Jesus spoke harshly against such motives (Matthew 6:5). Many relatively unknown people serve God humbly and with commitment—they are the "great" people in God's kingdom.

James and John eventually grew into servants without the need for special strokes from others. For that to happen, Jesus had to disciple them. He smoothed off the rough edges of their selfish attitudes with patience, correction, His own example, and by giving them opportunities for service.

We can more easily forget about ourselves when we are caught up in serving others. There are so many needs for God's disciples to meet. We should not even have time to think about what rung of the ladder we are on. Servant-kind of activities can free our minds of self-defeating thoughts of status.

## THEIR SPECIAL INVITATIONS TO LEARN

On three occasions, Jesus invited James and John (along with Peter) to participate in special experiences. One of those was the raising of Jairus' daughter from the dead (Mark 5:21-24, 35-43). There were many lessons for the disciples to learn from that one event: (1) Do not hold grudges. Jairus was a ruler in the synagogue. The synagogue leaders were behind much of the opposition to Jesus, but Jesus did not hold that against him. He simply thought of him as a man with a need. (2) Be willing to go beyond what is expected. Jairus had asked Jesus to heal his daughter of a sickness (Mark 5:23), but Jesus went much beyond that request. He raised her from the dead. (3) Be willing to do what is right and meet needs even though they may be laughed at. The people laughed at Jesus because they did not understand (Mark 5:40). (4) Realize that death is not the end. Just as Jesus raised the girl from the dead, He will also raise His followers. What a great truth for James and John to know, for within two years John was threatened (Acts 3, 4), and within ten years James was executed (Acts 12)!

James and John also participated in a most unique experience in Jesus' earthly life—the transfiguration (Matthew 17:1-8). Through that experience, they learned that no earthly men could outshine Jesus. It is fitting that Peter, James, and John would see this meaningful manifestation of Jesus because they were the disciples who were the most susceptible to the temptation to want to be the stars of the group. In the transfiguration the three of them clearly saw God overshadow Moses and Elijah (great stars of the past) and spotlight Jesus: "This is my Son, whom I love; with him I am well pleased. Listen to him!" (Matthew 17:5).

These disciples learned that they must not crowd out their commitment to Jesus by giving too much attention to worldly desires and ways of thinking. Peter was thinking in a worldly way when he said, "Lord, it is good for us to be here. If you wish, I will put up three shelters—one for you, one for Moses, and one for Elijah" (Matthew 17:4). Peter was putting men on a par with Jesus.

Any time we take our eyes off Jesus and become overly impressed with God's human servants, we need to remember the experience of the transfiguration. We must not consider Jesus to be just a man of the past. He is not in competition. He is the one of a kind!

The third invitation that Jesus gave to James and John (with Peter) was in the Garden of Gethsemane. He brought these three apart from the others to "keep watch with me" (Matthew 26:38). Jesus knew the cross was looming ahead; He wanted to spend time in prayer with His friends.

The three disciples fell asleep instead of keeping watch. But the graciousness of Jesus taught them that He understands that a disciple cannot stay on the go continuously. Jesus did not harshly rebuke them for resting. It is so easy for conscientious disciples today to feel guilty for resting. However, a disciple can take too much "relaxation"; thus to every disciple today Jesus' words are still relevant. "Watch and pray so that you will not fall into temptation. The spirit is willing, but the body is weak" (Matthew 26:41).

In later years, the disciples must have thought about throwing in the towel many times. Life got very rough for them, but they had learned from Jesus to let God have the final say. The moment we let our wills veto God's will for us, we have stepped out of the sandals of real discipleship.

## THEIR CHANGED LIVES

James and John became model disciples even though they were "stinkers" when Jesus called them to follow Him. James, who wanted to destroy opposition in great thunderous claps, calmed down and became gentle and caring under the teaching of Jesus. John, who had such a hot temper, wrote more about love than any other writer of the New Testament. He recorded Jesus' magnificent commission, "Love one another. As I have loved you, so you must love one another" (John 13:34). Only John recorded Jesus' saying, "Abide in My love" (John 15:9, NASB). Only John recorded Jesus' prayer that God's children be as united as Jesus is with the Father (John 17). John wrote two letters that commended people who loved (2 and 3 John). In 3 John he criticized a man who did not love as he should. In 1 John he developed the truth that love is one of the tests for determining whether or not a person is a Christian.

John became so compassionate and loving that Jesus committed the care of His mother to him (John

19:26). John went with Peter to show love to the Samaritans, whom John had earlier hated (Acts 8:14). John was one of the first to give Paul, the persecutor of Christians, the hand of fellowship (Galatians 2:9).

According to tradition, John was the only apostle who died a natural death. After being exiled to the isle of Patmos (an island used to punish criminals), John was given visions to encourage fellow Christians who were being persecuted because of their faith (Revelation 1:1, 4, 9; 21:2; 22:8). In his old age, John wrote a great victory letter. Instead of revengeful feelings when persecution came (as was his earlier reaction), John wrote about trusting God, who would bring history to an end in His own time and way. Instead of complaining, John wrote that we should join in a grand chorus to worship God (Revelation 4:8, 11; 5:9, 10, 13, 14; 7:16, 17; 11:15-18; 12:10-12; 15:3, 4; 16:7; 19:1-8).

Some historians tell us that John died at an old age (probably in his nineties) while living in Ephesus. He became so feeble that he had to be carried to the church assembly. He would regularly speak at the assembly, giving the same message: "Little children, love one another!" The people began to get tired of the repetition and asked him why he always gave the same message. John replied, "It is the Lord's command. And if this alone be done, it is enough."

Yes, the sons of thunder had become disciples of Jesus—and so can we!

# CHAPTER SEVEN

# A STUDY OF THE TWELVE: MATTHEW, THOMAS, JUDAS

## MATTHEW

Sometimes the church forgets about the "upper crust" of society and concentrates only on those who are "down and out." Why aren't more of the rich, the governmental officials, and the owners of industry in the church? We cannot dismiss it with a shrug of the shoulders or with a glib remark like, "Oh, they are too busy to care. They are wrapped up in financial concerns and have no time or interest to spare for the church." That is simply not true. Perhaps the church folk are so wrapped up in their insulated world that they have little time to care or to extend the invitation of Christ to the wealthy elite in the community.

Jesus loved the wealthy as well as the poor. He loved the unlovable, cared for the incurables, and touched the untouchables. He looked beyond a person's reputation to see His possibilities. And Jesus did not disciple by long-distance involvement; He became friends with those He discipled. Jesus' friendly type of discipleship method and His tendency to reach out to people in all walks of life is shown clearly in His relationship with Matthew.

Barclay calls Matthew "the man whom all men hated" *(Gospel of Matthew I,* Westminster Press, 1976, p. 330). He was a tax collector (publican), which meant he was a legalized crook. He was a rip-off artist for the government. He was a con man in a most lucrative business. The Roman government gave the business of collecting taxes to the highest bidder. A person had to be in the "upper crust" of society even to be considered for the job. And all the people in that culture knew the job was a political payoff.

Why would a person pay a high amount of money for a political appointment? One thing is certain—he did not do it to get poor. The government required that the collector turn in a certain amount of money. Any extra he received was his to use as he pleased. Thus every time a Jew turned around, he was being taxed. He was taxed for his produce, his income, his sex (a male paid a special tax just because he was a male), imports, exports, to travel on certain roads or bridges, for his animals, for his carts, a sales tax, and on and on the list goes. One historian said that it was not uncommon for a tax collector to receive $100,000 a year. That would be a lot of money today, but when the average day's pay was about twenty-five cents ($75 a year) such an amount for any one person was almost beyond imagination.

Tax collectors disadvantaged others to fill their own pockets. They did not care how poor people were as long as they themselves were getting richer. It is no surprise that the Jews hated them and even prohibited them from entering the synagogue. It would be logical to assume, then, that Jesus would ignore such men in order to be able to reach as many Jews as He could. To associate with a tax collector would certainly erect a barrier between Jesus and some of the people. However, Jesus did not succumb to the traditions or prejudices of men; He lived out God's will. As He passed by Matthew's den of iniquity—the tax collector's booth—He called Matthew to discipleship (Matthew 9:9).

What a laugh! Who would walk away from a powerful political position and an enormous income to travel around the countryside with a group of "crude" men learning from an itinerant teacher? Matthew did! He must have heard Jesus speak on several occasions. Perhaps he heard the people discuss this man from Nazareth who gave meaning to their lives. He must have come to realize that satisfaction in life does not come from riches but from what one is willing to give. Matthew had been a *taker* for too long. The invitation to follow Jesus was the new start in life that he needed.

Thus he moved from the elite politician's seat to the lowly seat of a pupil. He laid down the pen that kept track of tax payments to pick up the pen that recorded the life of Jesus, and in that action he made a positive contribution to the world for all eternity (he wrote the Gospel of Matthew). He walked away from a lucrative profession to receive much more in life.

Jesus did not complete the invitation to follow Him with just a onetime call. He followed up the call with a social visit. He did not want to be a teacher only to Matthew but also a friend. Jesus and His disciples had dinner at Matthew's house with him and other so-called "riff-raff" of the community ("many tax collectors and 'sinners,' " Matthew 9:10). What a disciple Matthew would be! Already he was introducing his sinful cronies to the sinless Jesus!

How could Jesus and His disciples attend such a dinner? Weren't they concerned about their reputations? Jesus was often criticized for associating with the wrong kind of people; His answer to His critics is classic:

> It is not the healthy who need a doctor, but the sick. But go and learn what this means: "I desire mercy, not sacrifice." For I have not come to call the righteous, but sinners (Matthew 9:12, 13).

Jesus knew that to disciple people He would have to become their friend.

The church must learn that same truth. We can never disciple people we don't like, and we will not like people with whom we refuse to associate. Making disciples involves taking the risk to reach out to the spiritually sick and healing them with a touch of the love of Christ.

In A.D. 252, a serious plague broke out in the city of Carthage. The plague was so devastating that as soon as a person became contaminated, his friends or family would throw him into the street to prevent the rest of the family from getting contaminated. No one dared touch the infested bodies of the living or dead. But one congregation went into the streets picking up the dead bodies to bury them and touching the sick to minister to them. The Christians who did these acts of kindness were called "gamblers" (risk-takers).

That kind of risk-taking has always been the job of the church. We must be willing not only to associate with the physically sick but also with the spiritually sick.

77

Jesus and His disciples were risking their reputations to reach out to those who needed the truths of God. That is what disciple making is all about.

Matthew's inclusion in the group of the twelve apostles is an amazing thing to observe. There is no hint that the other eleven derided him, ignored him, or backed away from him. He was accepted. He was "one of them."

Do we follow their example in our churches today? Are we friendly with the rich in our congregations? Or do we envy their financial standing and feel uncomfortable with them?

Some of Matthew's acceptance in the group probably resulted from his attitudes and actions as well as from the openness of the group. We can find no indication that he expected any special treatment because he had given up "so much" to follow Jesus. The church is filled with privileged people, but none is to be *the* privileged person. Part of discipling involves recognizing the truth and applying it.

History says that Matthew evangelized in several different countries and was stoned and beheaded. Discipleship was not always easy for him either.

## THOMAS

Although we know none of the details surrounding Jesus' calling of Thomas to discipleship, we know a little about Thomas as a person. He was a strange mixture of caution and courage.

His courage was seen when he alone stood against the other eleven disciples much as a general might stand in front of his troops and say, "Come on, boys, follow me." Jesus' crucifixion was drawing near. The apostles knew that Jerusalem was a "hot spot" of danger. When Jesus announced His plans to return there, the other eleven tried to change His mind— "But Rabbi . . . a short while ago the Jews tried to stone you, and yet you are going back there?" (John 11:8). Disciples of a teacher in that culture could expect whatever treatment their teacher received; so these men knew that if Jesus would be in danger in Jerusalem, they would be also.

When their first attempt to discourage Jesus from going to Jerusalem did not work, they tried another approach. They tried to persuade Jesus that a trip into the area would serve no practical purpose—"Lord, if he sleeps, he will get better" (referring to Lazarus, John 11:12). Their idea was, "Why go see Lazarus? He will be okay."

Thomas had listened to their line of reasoning long enough. He suddenly said, "Let us also go, that we may die with him" (John 11:16). Perhaps he so firmly believed that Jesus could raise Lazarus from the dead that he also believed that though they might die, they too would be raised. We do not know what was racing through the mind of Thomas, but we can observe that his response on this occasion was quite different from his reaction several days later.

Jesus needs disciples today who are willing to stick their necks out (yes, their lives) for Him. Disciples must not always choose the "secure" route. Growth can result as we step out on faith.

By the time we next hear of Thomas, the apostles had seen Jesus' wounded body and had seen Him stumble under the weight of the cross. They had heard the mallet drive the nails into His hands. They had seen Him die on the cross. They had seen Him wrapped for burial and placed in the tomb. They had seen the stone at the entrance sealed and the sentries arrive. Their beloved leader was dead. All their dreams and hopes could not change that fact.

The disciples were then meeting behind closed doors (John 20:19). They were living in fear; they no doubt started at every step they heard on the stairs outside the room. Were the soldiers coming after them?

Not long after Jesus' death, the women came saying Jesus had arisen! (Matthew 28:8). How could this be? The disciples refused to believe them, even Mary who said she had actually talked with Jesus (Mark 16:11). In fact, "their words appeared to them as nonsense" (Luke 24:11).

Even when they saw Jesus for themselves, they thought it must be a spirit (Luke 24:37). Jesus showed them His hands and feet and invited them to touch Him (24:39). That action also met with unbelief, but not a doubting unbelief. It was out of excitement and delight: "And while they still did not believe it for joy and amazement . . ." (24:41). I'm sure we can all understand their feelings. We have all reacted similarly when we encounter tremendous experiences and say, "I can't believe it!"

But this first time that Jesus appeared to the disciples, Thomas was absent. John makes a special point of noting Thomas' absence (John 20:24). Thomas has often been designated as the doubting disciple, but we can see that all of them doubted at first. Some have suggested that the problem with Thomas was not so much his skepticism as it was his absenteeism.

Significant things happen in the togetherness of God's people that cannot happen to one who wants to be a "lone ranger." The things that happen within the

80

fellowship of a congregation cannot be really appreciated by merely hearing a committee report on it.

The disciples tried to explain to Thomas what they had experienced, but he did not share their enthusiasm. He was cautious. It is interesting that the other disciples did not criticize Thomas' caution nor his previous absence. They did not turn their backs on him. There were apparently no under-the-breath innuendos or raised eyebrows that made Thomas feel that he would not be welcomed by the group eight days later than their first meeting. These men had been through too much together to allow this to cause a rift in their fellowship.

We can learn from this example that we need to be patient with one another. If people do not feel comfortable expressing doubts among us because we will cut them to pieces, we may be doing more to keep factions alive than to keep the fellowship united.

Thomas' courage was also seen in his caution. He again was willing to stand up against the crowd. He would not allow their position to become his in order to fit in with the group. He would not pretend he had no reservations about their story. He was honest.

I wonder how many times we sit in a Sunday-school class and clam up; we won't admit that we are puzzled about a teaching. The tragedy is that unless we get it out into the open, we may never be exposed to the evidence or explanation that might help us. If we all demanded more proof about what is taught as Thomas did, we could all look at the issues more honestly. We could see whether the teaching was really valid or needed to be changed, depending on the Biblical evidence.

Jesus did not condemn Thomas for his caution. Although He could have given him a verbal tongue-lashing for not believing, Jesus took the time to share the evidence with Thomas. He took the time to show Thomas what he wanted to see (John 20:25, 27). But Thomas did not need to touch Jesus; he saw and believed.

That was another positive thing about Thomas. When he did decide, he did not hedge. He did not rationalize or think about how foolish he might look to the others. He did not make excuses so he could hold on to his former position and save face.

Instead, Thomas immediately exclaimed Jesus was the Lord (John 20:28). He admitted that Jesus was the God of Israel. He was identifying Jesus with the Shema—the credal statement repeated in every synagogue service—"Hear O Israel: The Lord our God is one Lord" (Deuteronomy 6:4, see footnote). To the Jews, the Lord and God were the same.

Thomas was a courageous disciple though he had his doubts and was overly cautious at times. His life teaches us that we can find the truth if we honestly search and remain open to it. And Jesus' handling of Thomas shows us that patience and understanding is needed when discipling others.

## JUDAS ISCARIOT

Judas was one of the most popular names for Jewish boys in the first century (it means from Judah), but today few people would name their sons Judas because of the shame that is associated with this disciple of Jesus. Even though his name is repellent to us, we can learn some important truths about discipleship from him.

Although a disciple must associate with the right

teacher, the association does not guarantee that a good disciple will result. Judas sat at the feet of Jesus and heard His teachings as much as any of the other disciples, with the possible exception of Peter, James, and John; yet he was a failure.

The association with fellow disciples is also a very important part of discipleship, but having habitual contact with good people does not automatically result in a good person. Judas had daily fellowship with some of the finest people on earth; yet Satan had his way with him (Luke 22:3).

Judas also shows us that just because a disciple says he has the right concerns does not mean that he does. One time Judas became angry at what looked like a meaningless waste of precious perfume. Judas just about climbed the wall when Mary poured perfume worth a year's wages on Jesus' head and feet. He said, "Why wasn't this perfume sold and the money given to the poor?" (John 12:5). Many of us can see Judas' point and might agree with him.

What a man says, however, does not always communicate his motives: "He did not say this because he cared about the poor but because he was a thief; as keeper of the money bag, he used to help himself to what was put into it" (12:6). The verb "used to help" is misleading. It could sound as if he did that in the past but had quit. But the Greek tense of the verb designates that this was continuing action. Judas regularly and continually stole from the bag of money.

It is interesting to realize that Jesus knew what Judas was doing but still allowed him to manage the money for the group. No one can grow into mature discipleship unless he is trusted. Many times we stifle people's growth by not allowing them to do anything

83

without approval from some "higher-ups" on a board.

It is natural to want to "govern" people so tightly that no one can take advantage of us. But that would so overgovern that freedom would be taken away, and when freedom goes, so goes the spontaneous expression and growth of people. The Judases will appear now and then. We must not allow their arrival to trigger our reaction on our part. While Jesus lost one, the freedom He gave to His disciples helped develop the eleven others so that they turned the world upside down.

It is easy to slip into the idea that we can't let anyone loose with any of the church's money without prior approval and assurances of what the money is to be spent for. We often do the same thing with responsibilities. We find it hard to delegate them and find it even harder to allow people to run with their ideas unless the plans have been scrutinized and approved in detail beforehand. By doing this, we are failing to realize that the Spirit of God lives in all Christians, not just in the members of the board or Christian education committee. Jesus did not stifle his disciples, and neither should we.

Judas eventually betrayed Jesus for thirty pieces of silver. That was equal to a six-month's salary. When Judas saw the consequences of his action, he threw this large sum of money away. We know by this action that he had his regrets. But he did not carry that regret to repentance and ask for forgiveness. He threw his life away, instead. What a tragedy!

Jesus had poured months and months of His life and teachings into Judas, but He lost him to suicide. There is no guarantee that any teacher or leader will have 100 percent success. If a teacher or leader of the church loses someone to Satan, he can easily sink into despair and feel guilty. He asks, "Where did I fail?" But we must remember Judas. He had the finest teacher and associates, yet he failed. The teacher was not to blame. Each student (each disciple) has his own free will and makes his own decisions. We cannot force anyone to be good or to mature. That is a personal commitment and decision.

Judas also teaches us that regardless of how long we have been disciples, we cannot relax in our vigil to overcome sin. We must always be alert to the tricks of Satan. The idea of "once a disciple, always a disciple" is not Biblical. For the devil is like a lion who prowls around looking for persons to devour (1 Peter 5:8).

It is no wonder what the word "disciple" and the word "discipline" are so closely related. To be a disciple is to strive for maturity which involves self-control (discipline) and continued alertness. It involves never being smug or satisfied with one's present level of maturity. It is a complete awareness of all of Satan's powers.

# CHAPTER EIGHT

# PAUL

## PAUL, THE PHARISEE

Paul was a great disciple and disciple-maker, but his first experience with Christians was not with the idea to become one. Paul (Saul) was a strict traditional Jew. He admitted that he "was advancing in Judaism beyond many Jews of [his] own age and was extremely zealous for the traditions of [his] fathers" (Galatians 1:14). He said he had been "a Hebrew of Hebrews; in regard to the law, a Pharisee" (Philippians 3:5).

Paul was a rigid, hardhearted legalist who would not stand for anyone to try to change anything. He was the kind of person who put all of his energy behind whatever he was convinced was right. He did not compartmentalize his life, giving religion only one section. He linked his religion to every inch of his life. His religion affected his professional choices, his leisure time, his family, and his goals. Paul's theme song could have easily been, "I am determined. I have made up my mind. I will serve the Lord."

Not only was Paul clear about where he stood religiously, but other people knew as well. He was a major leader in Judaism. When he entered any synagogue, heads turned and people whispered, "There's Saul of Tarsus." People depended on him for direction. When the new Jesus movement began to catch fire, the people naturally turned to Paul for leadership. And Paul did not disappoint them. He led a devastating opposition movement against the Christians (Acts 8:1-3), beginning the day on which Stephen was stoned.

Paul's influence must have been extremely powerful, for he began the opposition in the very city in which the Christians had the most favorable reception with the people. Before Paul took over the leadership of the opposition, little had been done against the membership of the Christian group (except for Peter and John). The most powerful group of men in Jerusalem wanted to do more against the Christians, but they couldn't because "all the people were praising God for what had happened" (Acts 4:21). "The captain went with his officers and brought the apostles. They did not use force, because they feared that the people would stone them" (5:26). But when Paul led the opposition, the people backed him. He had more influence than the great court of the land (the Sanhedrin).

His influence was not confined to the local area either. After he succeeded in flushing out Christians from house to house and imprisoning them in Jerusalem (Acts 8:3), he received official backing to go to other cities for the same purpose (Acts 9:1, 2). Paul was not satisifed with simply putting Christians into jail; he was also interested in putting them into the grave. "Breathing out murderous threats" (9:1), he "persecuted the followers of this Way to their death" (Acts 22:4).

Paul had only one motive behind his actions: "I too was convinced that I ought to do all that was possible to oppose the name of Jesus of Nazareth" (Acts 26:9). Paul thought he was doing God a favor by defending the only religion that (Paul thought) God recognized—Judaism.

## PAUL, THE DISCIPLE

God was ready to use someone like Paul—someone who would act on his convictions, someone who would do what he believed to be the will of God regardless of the cost to himself. God weakened the opposition by winning their powerful leader to the cause of Christ. We are familiar with what happened to Paul on the road to Damascus (Acts 9, 22, 26), but we can discover some significant insights about discipleship by looking beyond what happened *to* Paul to what happened *in* Paul.

Although it appeared to all onlookers that Paul was inflexible, he wasn't. He still remained open to doing God's will no matter what God asked of him, even if it meant reversing a lifelong way of thinking. Being able to change, as we have pointed out in other chapters, is so important to a growing disciple of Jesus.

It is very threatening to be asked to reverse a stance you have held for a long time and been very vocal about. The natural tendency is to defend that view until the day you die. Many of us make up our minds on an issue and then close our minds to any further discussion. We think that settles the question forever. We have examined the facts and are sure that things never change. We are sure that we are right, and we expect God to defend our position. In fact, we might even teach God a few things about it. How arrogant!

But Paul was not like that. He was teachable. He could be influenced. We can discover many ways in which Paul changed by reading his writings. Consider the chart on the next page.

| Traditional View | Paul's New View |
|---|---|
| A man may divorce for any reason. | Husbands should not put away their wives (1 Corinthians 7:11); wives are bound to their husbands for life (7:39). |
| The Jerusalem temple is the only place for worship. | The body is the temple of the Spirit (1 Corinthians 6:19). |
| Prejudiced against the Gentiles. | There is no difference between Jew and Greek (Galatians 3:28). |
| It is necessary for one to be a Jew physically. | If one belongs to Christ, he is of Abraham (Galatians 3:29). |
| Circumcision is necessary. | Circumcision is not by the letter, but of the heart, by the Spirit (Romans 2:29). |
| The law makes one righteous. | Righteousness is not derived from the law, but from faith in Christ (Philippians 3:9). |
| The church should be destroyed. | The wisdom of God is manifested through the church (Ephesians 3:10). |
| Christ was a sinner. | He was without sin, but became sin on our behalf (Hebrews 4:15; 2 Corinthians 5:21). |
| Christ was a liar. | The truth is in Jesus (Ephesians 4:21). |
| Christ was possessed by demons. | If one does not have the Spirit of Christ, he can not belong to Him (Romans 8:9). List of fruits of the Spirit (Galatians 5:22 ff). |

Paul also changed his whole way of leading people. Jesus spoke about the type of leadership the Pharisees provided: "They tie up heavy loads and put them on men's shoulders, but they themselves are not willing to lift a finger to move them" (Matthew 23:4). But after Paul became a Christian, he exposed himself to all kinds of heavy loads so he could help others lift them. He wrote about working with his own hands so as not to be a burden to others (2 Thessalonians 3:8).

Paul knew what it meant to be flogged, to be beaten with rods, to be stoned and left for dead, to be shipwrecked, to go without sleep, without food, and without clothes (2 Corinthians 11:23-27). He lived out his commitment so completely that he could say, "So I will very gladly spend for you everything I have and expend myself as well" (2 Corinthians 12:15). What a change from a Pharisee who had many advantages in life and who burdened down others!

Are we willing to change? Is our expression of discipleship the same now as it was a few years ago? Are we putting ourselves out for others? Or have we slipped into a comfortable routine?

Pharisees were also known to do things in order for others to see them and praise them (Matthew 23:5). But Paul put that characteristic behind him. He once said, "So then, men ought to regard us as servants of Christ ..." (1 Corinthians 4:1). The word for "servant" in that verse tells volumes about Paul. It is the Greek word (uperetas) that described the underrowers who worked without honor underneath the decks of a ship. They were below the deck sweating and tired, moving the oars to a command. They did it so others could reach their destinations. They got callouses but no credit; they got fatigue but no flowers.

That is what discipleship includes. Paul moved from living as a Pharisee to living as a disciple; we must be careful that we don't move from living as a disciple to living as a Pharisee.

Jesus said the Pharisees loved "to be greeted in the market place and to have men call them 'Rabbi' " (Matthew 23:7). Paul was almost certainly hooked on his titles before he became a Christian, but afterwards he said he was seen as a "spectacle" (1 Corinthians 4:9). What kind of spectacle? "The scum of the earth, the refuse of the world" (1 Corinthians 4:13). How many leaders in the church today are willing to be called garbage? We put our degrees, awards, and honors on our walls; we put our degrees behind our names on our stationery; we will take any type of course in a college just to have the title of Doctor. We love to put our pictures in the newspapers and have buildings named after us. Where is our humility and our attitude of lowly service?

For Paul discipleship was synonymous with the word *service*. He lived to serve the needs of others in the name of Jesus. He preached, taught, wrote, traveled, visited, wept, prayed, and trained others to carry on his work—all with a view to helping others mature in the faith.

And he did it without fanfare. He spoke in tongues, but never bragged about it (1 Corinthians 14:18). He had received special instruction from the Lord, but he never sent out press releases announcing how he had talked with God in some sensational way (Galatians 1:12). He never asked people to send him money so he could build an expensive cathedral. He asked for money with which to feed the poor (2 Corinthians 8, 9) and to help spread God's message. He named no

91

association after himself. In fact, he admitted that he was the "least of the apostles and [did] not even deserve to be called an apostle" (1 Corinthians 15:9).

Paul had every reason to be a "lone ranger" disciple—to do it alone without the fellowship of other disciples. He had had experiences that they had not had. He could have seen himself as someone special; after all, God called him to a particular mission. But Paul knew that the contribution of the whole body of Christ to an individual disciple and the contribution of the individual disciple to the body are indispensible to God's cause. He made it a point to fellowship with others (Galatians 1:18; Acts 9:19, 26). He did not work just *for* the church, but also *within* the church (Acts 11:25-27). He traveled because the Holy Spirit *through* the church sent him, not because he decided to strike out on his own (Acts 13:1-3). He felt such a responsibility to the church at Antioch that he returned with reports and to engage in a mutual ministry with her (Acts 14:26-28). No disciple of Christ today should feel he is "special" or that he can do it all by himself. We all need the encouragement, strength, and spiritual guidance that other disciples can give us.

Some historians record that Paul was beheaded near Rome on the same day that Peter was crucified. But Paul was prepared for such an event as he wrote, "For to me, to live is Christ and to die is gain" (Philippians 1:21).

## PAUL, THE DISCIPLE-MAKER

Because Paul was so committed to working on a team, he committed himself to making disciples as well as to being one. Paul's focal point of serving was either to bring people into the discipleship role initially or to mature them as disciples (Colossians 1:28, 29). Much of his writings were for the purpose of developing disciples within the churches (Romans 12—16; 1 Corinthians 12—14; Ephesians 4:11-16).

Paul not only sought to develop disciples through the "mass" method of writing and preaching, but also by the "individual" method of teaching a person one-on-one. There is probably an endless list of individuals that Paul discipled personally. Many, though not all, of the individuals listed in Acts 18:1; 20:4; Philippians 2:25; 2 Timothy 4:10-13, 19-21; 1 Timothy 1:20; and Romans 16 would no doubt be on such a list. Paul was continually making disciples.

Timothy is the best example of Paul's ability to mold a disciple. Paul picked up a young man who was a "nobody" beyond his immediate locality and made him into an international somebody to be used by God. Timothy was an unlikely candidate because he was from a religiously and racially mixed family (Acts 16:1). He was also frequently sick with stomach problems (1 Timothy 5:23). But Paul did not let Timothy's background or his ailments blind him to Timothy's potential.

Paul saw in Timothy's disposition the kind of balance Paul knew his evangelistic team needed. Paul was the type of person who would enter a city walking, but have to come out running. He would enter as an unknown but come out well known. If anyone would be thrown in jail, it would be Paul. Timothy, on the other hand, was more quiet and calm. Paul would be beaten and thrown in prison, but Timothy would escape such treatment (Acts 16:22-40). In Thessalonica, some Christians had to post bond, probably to insure that Paul would not come to that city again. And as far as we know, he didn't. But Timothy was able to stay behind at that time and was able to return later (1 Thessalonians 3:1, 2).

Paul knew he could send Timothy to a troubled church or to a church whose membership was divided because of their differing loyalty to Paul (1 Corinthians 1:12; 16:10-12). He knew that Timothy would stay in a location and patiently work through the problems (1 Timothy 1:3-7). Many of Paul's letters include a greeting from Timothy probably because he knew that Timothy's reception in that church would be good (2 Corinthians 1:1; Philippians 1:1; Colossians 1:1; 1 Thessalonians 1:1; 2 Thessalonians 1:1).

What does this teach us about disciple-making? It teaches us that we should not overlook people just because they are different from us. We should allow a person to use his abilities in ministries that he can do the best, not give him the jobs we don't want to do. It may be more beneficial to allow a person to serve awhile in many different areas to discover his disposition, his interests, and his abilities before we lock him into a certain position or committee or before we burden him down with a job description. If we are more flexible, we may find areas of need being met when we didn't even know they existed. And we may discover new and exciting fulfillment in serving as various members in the body of Christ. We must remember that the church should be run as God would run it, not like a business.

Every member in the church is a minister—paid or unpaid. How are we using them? Are we putting people on committees and into services in which they have no interest but feel compelled to serve because they were asked to? If so, it is no wonder some people feel more fulfilled using their talents outside the structure of the church than through the church. We must free people to use their present abilities and dispositions for the body of Christ.

For instance, what if you have a banker in your church? Should you put him on the "building and grounds" committee? Instead, why not allow him to counsel church families concerning their budgeting or financial problems? Or perhaps there is a couple who have no children of their own but who love children and can really get excited about youth work. Then why not equip them by sending them to youth conferences and conventions and by providing them with sponsor training?

Paul's relationship with Timothy can also teach us about relationships between ministers (paid or unpaid). Paul had every right to call himself the "senior" minister over Timothy (there is nothing wrong with the title, but it should not be used to designate superiority). Instead Paul called himself Timothy's father (1 Corinthians 4:17; 1 Timothy 1:2). What a beautiful way to describe a relationship! Not a boss-employee relationship, but a father-son relationship.

Paul protected Timothy (1 Corinthians 16:10, 11; 2 Corinthians 1:19; Acts 16:3) and equipped Timothy by letting him be with him in all kinds of situations. He exposed him to all dimensions of experience and allowed Timothy to perform a significant ministry. He bragged about Timothy by calling him a "fellow worker" (Romans 16:21) and a "brother" (2 Corinthians 1:1). He said, "He is carrying on the work of the Lord, just as I am" (1 Corinthians 16:10); "I have no one else like him, who takes a genuine interest in your welfare" (Philippians 2:20); "But you know that

95

Timothy has proved himself . . . he has served with me in the work of the gospel'' (2:22). When Paul was quite advanced in years, he wrote at least two personal letters to Timothy urging him to keep on serving (1 and 2 Timothy). What a delight it must have been to be trained by Paul!

Paul's success with Timothy was not in his efforts to change him. Timothy was still probably timid (2 Timothy 1:7). But Paul's success was seen in the many ways Timothy served the churches and in his care and concern for people. Paul said, ''I have no one else like him'' (Philippians 2:20). The Greek literally reads— ''For I have no one equally souled.'' Paul said he and Timothy were equally souled in the way they genuinely cared for the welfare of others. They both cared for Christ's interests, not their own (Philippians 2:20-22).

Before we call a representative from our churches a ''Timothy'' of the church in a certain field of service, perhaps we should wait and see whether that person develops a compassion for people and their needs, to see whether he becomes ''equally souled'' with Christ. Anyone who spends his days caring for others, whether he leaves the church to go into other fields or not, should be considered the church's ''Timothy.'' Anyone can grow as a disciple in this way whether he is paid or not.

Are we developing Timothys in our church? Are you acting as a Timothy in your own ministry? It will not happen overnight, but it can happen. It just takes disciple-makers like Paul to do it.

CHAPTER NINE

# JESUS, THE DISCIPLE-MAKER

Disciples are not born; they are made. Making disciples requires time, but not time alone. Jesus shows us by His example the dimensions that are involved in disciple-making, and we can apply them to our efforts today.

## ASSOCIATION WITH PURPOSE

Jesus knew that if twelve men with different backgrounds, dispositions, personalities, and interests were to become disciples of His instead of disciples of their own self-interests, they would have to spend time with Him in close association. Thus when He chose the twelve to become His personal disciples, He did it for the initial purpose "that they might be with him" (Mark 3:14).

Have you ever heard the theory that parenting children requires qualitative time, not quantitive time? It sounds good, but it is not true. It is simply an excuse or rationalization for not spending much time with children. We don't expound that theory about anything else we are seeking to develop. A farmer would not apply that theory to his work; he knows that doing his work well requires a great deal of time each day. We do not use that theory if we wish to develop a talent. We would not say that a few minutes a day will make us great pianists even if that time was of great quality. I would not tell my children that they could learn to play ball with five minutes a day of qualitative instruction. It takes much time, association, and practice to develop anything or anyone worthwhile—our work, our talents, our children, *and disciples.*

If we are seeking for quality of time in developing children or disciples, our time will be carefully structured and planned. But children and disciples learn the most from us in the day-by-day, run-of-the-mill, routine experiences. It is in those non-planned, spontaneous experiences that they learn who we really are. We need *both* the quality of time and the quantity of time when developing others.

Thus Jesus did not call the twelve to be with Him for a few hours a day in a planned, classroom-type experience. He called them to be with Him through all the unplanned encounters that He would face in His ministry. In this way, the disciples truly learned Jesus' way of thinking and responding. When Jesus said, "Come and see" (John 1:39), "Follow me" (John 1:43), and "Learn from me" (Matthew 11:29), He was in part saying, "I'm calling you to discipleship in an intimate association with me."

Jesus took His disciples with Him on retreats, on trips to cities, to the marketplace, on fishing boats, to the synagogue, to the temple, to a funeral, to a wedding, to the sick, to parties, and to the remote countryside. They walked together, visited friends together, sailed together, vacationed together, ate together, slept together, prayed together, worshiped together, cried together, and laughed together. They talked about their past heritage in Judaism, the Scriptures, the signs of the time, the future, the world around them, fishing, and Jesus' teachings. Jesus used the unexpected moments to teach, utilizing what was close at hand—an event, a scene just viewed, an aspect of nature, or things that the disciples saw and experienced everyday (such as flowers, birds, salt, seed, leaven, light, pearls, and fishing.).

The disciples saw Jesus early in the morning, in the quiet hours of the evening, in the hot hours of the afternoon, and even late into the night. They observed what He was like after spending the night in the mountains praying. They observed His reactions when people disagreed with His teachings or when people thronged just to touch Him. They saw Him when He was rested and when He was tired. They saw Him when He was hungry and when He was full. They saw Him happy as well as when He was grieving. They observed His attitudes when He was with women and children, with the rich and the poor, and with the sick and the well. They saw him respond to religious leaders, to the immoral, to the Jews, and to the Gentiles. They noted His attitudes toward His family, friends, and strangers. Yes, Jesus spent a great quantity of time with His disciples.

What was Jesus' purpose for this close association? First, He wanted them to know Him as He was, and to become like Him (Luke 6:40). Secondly, He wanted them to learn how to preach and minister to people's needs (Mark 3:14; Matthew 10:7, 8).

Jesus was not only interested in His disciples' preaching ability or in how they could meet needs. He was just as concerned about *who* they were becoming. He wants the service of all of His disciples to flow out of their inner characters. He wants our *doing* to come out of our *being*.

It is not too difficult to teach others how to preach or teach. It is much more difficult and important to teach how to live. That is what is necessary in making disciples of Jesus.

## DEMONSTRATION

But close association is not all there is to discipling others. It is too easy for "discipling groups" to spring up and narrow discipling to just associating with a few people very closely. Some of these groups spend their time "sharing" and letting all their feelings "hang out." They usually turn into selfish therapy groups or into cliques that alienate all those not included in the group. Why? Because they do not expand their horizons or include a study of the life of Jesus or see a clear demonstration of a Christlike life.

Jesus' association with His disciples was not just "togetherness." He also taught by demonstrating clearly what it meant to live His way. He demonstrated that we must not get locked into traditions just for traditions' sake (Matthew 9:14-17). He demonstrated how to react when we are laughed at (9:24). He demonstrated that we should not get hooked on any one method of doing things. Jesus showed different ways of healing and ministering to people. He demonstrated many different ways of communicating. His sermons were varied—topical, expositional, exegetical, devotional, and theological.

I have heard many times, "The only sermon that is Biblical is such and such kind." But through Jesus' own example we can see that many different kinds can be used to communicate certain types of content to certain groups of people. When we restrict ourselves to certain ways of doing things, we are probably becoming a disciple of a method rather than a disciple of the Master. Much disunity in Christianity has its rootage in just such misplaced discipleship.

By Jesus' demonstrations the disciples learned so much—how to pray, how to use Scripture, the importance of fellowship, how to express fellowship, the importance of teaching, how to teach, the importance of compassion and how to express it, and how to disciple others. By close examination and study of the Scriptures, we can learn the same important truths and principles from Jesus' example.

## DELEGATION

Jesus did not stop with association or with demonstrations; He also delegated responsibilities to the twelve. Someone has said, "Impression without expression is void." Jesus was not interested in keeping His disciples in an eternal classroom without ever applying what they had been taught. He was not interested in enlisting soldiers to spend their entire career in "boot camp."

If a baby bird will not leave the nest to fly, the mother bird will disturb the nest so much that the little bird is literally "kicked out." The message is "fly or fall." Jesus did much the same thing to His twelve disciples when He told them to get out into the world and minister as He had been doing.

But Jesus was patient. He did not force them to leave the "nest" before they were prepared to do so. He did not have the philosophy, "We must put them to work immediately." Thus He did not assign tasks to them for quite a long time after He had called them.

Neither did He throw cold water on their spontaneous efforts of service. Some went out immediately and brought others to Him. At the same time He did not expect all of the disciples to do that.

Jesus gave them the mundane (as we would call them) tasks as well as the spectacular ones. At times the disciples would prepare, purchase, and distribute food. They would prepare a banquet room, obtain a donkey, pay taxes, go fishing for food, arrange housing accommodations, row a boat, or simply wait for Jesus. And guess what? Not once do we find a disciple saying, "That is not my charisma," or "That is not what I left my business to do," or "I did not spend my time studying under Jesus to do *this!*" or "This is work for a servant, not me."

Jesus delegated this wide range of responsibilities so His disciples would realize that there was nothing too insignificant for them to do or nothing too great for them to handle. If Jesus were discipling ministers today, I imagine He would spend time showing them how to run the mimeograph machine, how to sweep out a fellowship hall, how to shovel snow off sidewalks, and how to be careful to turn off the lights after everyone has left the church building. Of course, we don't want to burden our ministers down with a multitude of trivial duties; he must have time for study of the Word and for prayer (Acts 6:1-4). But no minister should think such tasks are *beneath* him.

### INSTRUCTION

The disciples of Jesus learned from close association with Him, from observing demonstrations of His life and attitudes, from doing what He delegated for them, and from His specific teachings to others and to them.

Jesus felt special teaching sessions (structured classroom type) were important. At times the twelve invited such sessions by asking questions. Some of Jesus' finest teachings came from instances when He was answering His disciples' questions (Matthew 17:10-13; 24; Mark 9:28, 29; 10:10; Luke 8:9-15). On other occasions, the disciples' arguing among themselves brought about a teaching session (Luke 22:24-29). He also taught them at meal times (John 13—16). Sometimes Jesus would ask questions and teach from their answers (Matthew 16:13-20). In many instances, He allowed a particular situation to be the springboard for a lecture (Matthew 11:1-19; 19:13-15; Luke 15). Sometimes Jesus used a statement made by one of the twelve as an introduction to a lesson (Mark 10:28-31). At other times Jesus purposely got the twelve off by themselves for a special teaching session (Mark 4:34; 9:30, 31).

## IMPARTATION

The continuation of Jesus' character and conduct in the lives of His disciples would be a result of their imitating Jesus as well as what Jesus would impart to them. He promised to put into their lives the Spirit of God. On the night on which He was betrayed, Jesus promised not to leave them alone but to send God's Spirit to live within them (John 14:16-23). The Holy Spirit would so live in these men that they could enjoy unity with God the Father and Jesus the Son after Jesus would physically be gone (John 17).

Jesus did not only want to impress these men with His life and message; He also wanted to impart unto them His very essence. That is the reason He promised them His peace (John 16:33), His joy (15:11), His love (15:9), His power (Matthew 10:8; Acts 1:8), His sanctification (John 17:17), His death (Matthew 20:22), and His future (John 14:1, 2).

Jesus equipped His disciples inwardly so they could function as they should outwardly. There is no such thing for a disciple of Jesus as not having the Holy Spirit within and not being united with Jesus. Only as Jesus imparted himself to those twelve could He say, "Remain in me, and I will remain in you" (John 15:4). Only in that oneness could Jesus have prayed, "As you sent me into the world, I have sent them into the world" (John 17:18).

Do you want to be a disciple of Jesus? Then you must be converted and be united with Him. You must be yoked with Jesus, not just look at Him or learn from Him. This is Jesus' initial invitation to discipleship: "Come to me, all you who are weary and burdened, and I will give you rest. Take my yoke upon you and learn from me, for I am gentle and humble in heart, and you will find rest for your souls" (Matthew 11:28, 29).

The disciple of Jesus can find rest for his soul because unity with Jesus reconciles (brings close) him to the Father. No one is at rest who is alienated from God. And no one who is not reconciled to the Father is a disciple of Jesus, for Jesus himself said, "I am the way and the truth and the life. No one comes to the Father except through me" (John 14:6).

Discipleship and disciple-making do not only bless us in this life on earth; the effects benefit us for eternity. Our orders include the eternal promise of association with Jesus—forever.

All authority in heaven and on earth has

been given to me. Therefore go and make disciples of all nations, baptizing them in the name of the Father and of the Son and of the Holy Spirit, and teaching them to obey everything I have commanded you. And surely I will be with you always, to the very end of the age (Matthew 28:18-20).

Thus both the call to discipleship (Mark 3:14) and the last promise Jesus gave to His disciples are the same—to be *with* Jesus. That is what it means to be a disciple of Jesus.

# CHAPTER TEN

# MAKING DISCIPLES TODAY

The marching orders for the church begin with the Great Commission (Matthew 28:18-20). Too many times we begin quoting the Great Commission, "Therefore, go. . . ." It begins not with what we are to do, however, but with who Jesus is, "All authority in heaven and on earth has been given to me." We go because the One with authority tells us to go. In fact, our submission to His authority tests our discipleship.

What are we to do as we go? We are to do three things: (1) make disciples of all nations, (2) baptize them, (3) and teach them to obey what Jesus commands. Whom are we to baptize? We are to baptize the disciples we have made. That means we must so introduce people to Jesus that they decide to follow Him before we baptize them. Sometimes we are guilty of baptizing people in the hope that they will become disciples of Jesus. Doing it that way is backwards. A person becomes a disciple by trusting Jesus enough (faith) to turn from what he *was* following to Jesus (repentance). It is the disciple who is baptized into Christ, not just anyone whom we grab off the street.

Then we must *teach* the baptized disciples. What are we to teach them? *Everything* Jesus commanded. Perhaps one reason so many preachers and teachers receive so much static is that they spend too much time teaching Jesus' commands to the wrong people. A person who is not a disciple and has not put on Christ in baptism (Galatians 3:26, 27) will often balk at being taught Jesus' commands. But the baptized disciple who has the Holy Spirit within Him (Acts 2:38; 2 Peter 1:4) wants to be taught everything Jesus commanded. We are to teach them also to *obey* Jesus' commands—not just to know them, or be able to list them, or be able to discuss them, or to memorize them. We are to enable the disciples to grow up into Christlikeness.

How do we do it? God has told us. He has structured the church in such a way that certain people equip others to do the

> works of service, so that the body of Christ may be built up until we all reach unity in the faith and in the knowledge of the Son of God and become mature, attaining to the whole measure of the fullness of Christ. Then we will no longer be infants, tossed back and forth by the waves, and blown here and there by every wind of teaching and by the cunning and craftiness of men in their deceitful scheming. Instead, speaking the truth in love, we will in all things grow up into him who is the Head, that is, Christ. From him the whole body, joined and held together by every supporting ligament, grows and builds itself up in love, as each part does its work (Ephesians 4:12-16).

There are three primary dimensions in this plan of God: (1) the church matures as each person works, (2) each person works as he is prepared to do so, and (3) maturing of the disciples means the church will not be swayed or destroyed by every theological fad that comes along.

## DISCIPLESHIP METHODS

Recently Christianity seems to have rediscovered the concept of discipleship. The current movement has both negative and positive sides. The positive side is that we are taking seriously the need to make true disciples and in that way are following the example of Jesus, the examples of the apostles, and the marching orders of the church. The negative aspect has been the insistence by some that one certain method is the only method of discipleship.

Some individuals have chosen the one-to-one method, which involves meeting with a person on a one-to-one basis over a long period of time in order to pour into that person as much as the "teacher" can. Often these meetings are in the early morning hours over breakfast. The teacher decides what he wants to share with his "disciple."

Others use the classroom approach. This involves a group of people joining a certain class or cell group with established goals. When a person finishes the class, he moves on to another cell that has another group of goals. Thus he matures and advances from cell to cell. When he progresses from the leadership class, he will be in charge of his own cell and teach others. In this way, the cells are continuously multiplying throughout the church.

A cell group usually consists of six to ten people who make a commitment to that group for a certain period of time. At each group meeting a different member is the leader. His responsibility is not to run the meeting but to be the catalyst that encourages discussion and keeps it flowing, while making certain everyone is drawn into the discussion. The meeting begins with a few minutes of silent meditation. The next five minutes are spent in prayer. Bible study and discussion follow. Each member seeks for specific ways to implement what was learned in the Bible study and commits himself to applying the truths. After the set period of time is over, the people regroup or form another group.

Others prefer the chain-of-command approach. This approach involves having each member being submitted to someone and all being responsible for each other.

Some churches have adopted the shepherding approach. Shepherds are selected from the membership, and the whole congregation is divided by family units into flocks with a shepherd assigned to each flock. The discipling of that flock becomes the responsibility of that shepherd. The shepherd is contacted by the church office or members of the flock when a member of his flock is absent, becomes ill, has a problem, or has a special joy to share. The shepherd goes to the homes of his flock members on a regular basis and seeks to become well acquainted with them. Sometimes the midweek service is a type of ''flock night,'' for each flock meets together for prayer and teaching by the shepherd.

Then there are many churches who use the traditional approach of having small Bible-school classes, periodic socials, worship services, and a midweek service; and through this approach they disciple many. It is interesting to observe many who have left this latter traditional method and who verbally throw stones at it—yet that was the method that discipled them! To grow beyond a certain method that we have been exposed to does not mean that method is wrong. In fact, that method must have worked well to allow others the freedom to search out new methods.

Discipling cannot be reduced to any one "infallible" method. God has given us freedom in methodology. A wide variety of approaches is available and useful. But there are some dangers to watch out for.

(1) Do not establish one method as the only method for the church. People are different; not all will like one certain approach.

(2) The church leadership should not be threatened by people's meeting in groups outside the church building. If the only way people will "stay in line" is by keeping them in one place under supervision, then chaos will reign during the week when they are scattered. To make a rule that Christians of the church cannot meet in someone's home during the week is to use Diotrephes' approach (read 3 John). We must trust that God's Word and the Holy Spirit can do more positive good with people than authoritarian demands.

(3) Sometimes there is a tendency for the cell groups (or similar groups) to become so "clannish" that they set themselves apart from others of the church and start comparing their group with other groups. Some who have started what they call "discipling groups" imply that anyone who is not in such a group is an inferior Christian. Such attitudes divide the body of Christ into factions and do not promote the growth of the disciples.

(4) A cell group should not use its time to discuss the church or the people in the church. Griping or criticizing or gossiping are not steps to maturing as disciples. No mature disciple will engage in judging

others. Every group and member in the group must maintain humility and love. We should follow the admonition of Paul:

> We who are strong ought to bear with the failings of the weak and not to please ourselves. Each of us should please his neighbor for his good, to build him up (Romans 15:1, 2).

(5) Each group should try to be a service group, actively seeking to reach out and contribute. But in each avenue of service the whole church should be invited and allowed to participate lest others outside the group think the discipling group is becoming a clique by wanting to do everything in the church.

## CHURCH PROGRAMMING

The leaders of the church should constantly be evaluating the program of the church with the maturing of the disciples in mind. Some activities may need to be discontinued, others may need some adjustment, and others may need to be added. We should never become more attached to programs than to our purpose of growth and evangelism. Since the church is the body of Christ, she should use some of the main dimensions that Jesus and Paul used when discipling others:

(1) *PERSONAL ASSOCIATION.* Close association among the disciples is a must in the life of the church. Too often people come into the church and have to grow up into Christ by themselves, except for the regular, scheduled meetings, because no one really cares enough about them to help in their growth. There is no substitute for close fellowship of the disciples and

the teachers. This fellowship does not always have to be specifically planned or be in the church building. Christians need to spend time with each other in homes, on excursions, eating out together, attending conferences, and other available opportunities.

(2) *DEMONSTRATION.* One person who has a ministry should ask another person to go with him and help. The ministry may be visiting nursing homes, hospitals, the shut-ins, going evangelistic calling, visiting newcomers in town, manual labor for the elderly, or cooking for a widower. In this way another person is learning about a service ministry by observing how it is done. Of course, selecting "interns" should be done after much prayer and consideration of interests and abilities.

(3) *DELEGATION.* One person in the church should not be expected to "do it all." Responsibilities must de delegated. After the delegation those who have responsibilities should be supported, helped in every possible way, and lifted up for appreciation. I know of a preacher who has committed himself to visit in the home of every Sunday-school teacher at least once a year to encourage them and express appreciation.

(4) *INSTRUCTION.* The church should be continuously evaluating her teaching program. Are there needs that the present curriculum is not meeting? Could electives be offered to reach more people? How about using videotaped lessons? I know of one church that offers a videotape lesson at 7 A.M. on a weekday for those who cannot participate at night. Do the members need a special class? Should classes be offered for the handicapped? Shouldn't there be a continuous teacher-training program?

(5) *LIBERATION*. Each disciple has tremendous power locked up inside of him in the form of talents or abilities. God has given every person abilities that can contribute to the body of Christ and to a needy world. The church should seek to unlock those attributes and encourage their use. One approach involves a study of God's purpose, God's call, a look at the needs around us, and discovering the resources within the church to meet those needs. A helpful guide to such a study is *Discovering My Gifts for Service* by Standard Publishing.

## DISCIPLING WITHIN THE FAMILY UNIT

It may be that the best place to disciple people has been overlooked. I feel the best place to implement all the aspects of discipling is in the home. The family is the discipling group that God gives to every parent. Parents dare not forsake their children while they attend church meetings or cell group get-togethers every night of the week. A discipling group of the church should not be in competition for the time that is needed for the family unit's togetherness—a natural discipling group.

It is only within the family that people can observe one another in every type of human experience—recreation, joy, grief, shame, patience, while on vacation, working, and eating. As the children observe the parents in all these experiences, they are being discipled as were the twelve who observed Jesus so closely.

It is within the family unit that every one of the admonitions in the New Testament can be expressed without necessitating planned and organized programs. The family can have a close-knit group without

113

becoming a clique or posing a threat to the rest of the church. The church expects a family to eat together, go on trips together, and sit together during worship; but cell groups or discipling groups who do so can sometimes cause a negative reaction among the other church members, and factions can result.

## CONCLUSION

Discipleship means the total church as the body of Christ will be involved in the total ministry of Christ. It does not mean we will be patting ourselves on the back because we have discovered a new approach or new fad. Discipleship is not new. Discipleship is not unusual. Discipleship does not depend on gimmicks or the sensational. Neither is it an impossible dream. It is real. It is necessary. It is becoming like Jesus. It is living to serve others, not living to be served. It is giving our all with persistence and dedication. It is living lives of obedience. It is receiving the blessings, the promises, and the eternal reward.

Come . . . Follow . . . Learn . . . Grow . . . Teach others . . . Be a disciple of Jesus!

# PRINCIPLES OF DISCIPLESHIP

## BEING DISCIPLES

*Goal:* To imitate Jesus

*First Step:* Be united with Jesus

*Characteristics:*
1. Teachable, growing
2. Humble
3. Free from selfishness
4. Patient
5. Obedient
6. Serving others
7. Desiring to have Christ seen through you
8. Prayerful
9. Seeking righteousness
10. Fully committed
11. Realizing the cost
12. Ready without hesitation
13. Stable in faith
14. Compassionate
15. Self-controlled
16. Forgiving
17. Free of prejudice
18. Bringing others to Jesus
19. Honest

## MAKING DISCIPLES

*Goal:* Develop Christlikeness in others

*First Step:* Be a disciple yourself

*Actions:*
1. Have objective clearly in mind
2. Realize difference between crowds and disciples
3. Be patient; realize that growth takes time
4. Consider everyone as a prospect
5. Select disciples for potential, not perfection
6. Teach about both privilege and purpose
7. Allow flexibility and freedom
8. Be a friend
9. Provide close fellowship
10. Provide discipline
11. Provide Bible instruction
12. Provide learning experiences
13. Delegate responsibility
14. Be a good example of Christlikeness
15. Take risks for the benefit of others
16. Realize that failure is possible

More Books for
# Christian Growth
by Knofel Staton

**Discovering My Gifts for Service** presents a satisfying approach to helping each church member become aware of his unique gifts, and of the many opportunities the church affords for using those gifts to serve the Lord.

**Grow, Christian, Grow.** The spectacular stories of some very unlikely New Testament persons and how they grew spiritually. A challenging elective study for young people and adults.

**How to Know the Will of God.** What is God's will? How can you find out what He wants you to do? There are ways of finding God's guidance for the problems of everyday life. Some of them are presented in this book.

**How to Understand the Bible.** Easy-to-use Bible study tools for the layman. Step-by-step lessons, plus discussions of topics, words, customs and contexts. For individual or class study.

**Check Your Lifestyle.** Step-by-step guidelines on how to make the principles of Proverbs come to life in the 20th century. A painfully practical book that moves Christianity into the "nitty-gritty" of daily living. For class or individual study.

**Check Your Character.** A soul-searching study of the Beatitudes—"the beautiful attitudes of Jesus"—in the Sermon on the Mount. The Beatitudes explain Jesus' sometimes perplexing behavior. And they explain the rightness of the same behavior for us, for today. Each chapter ends with questions to check your motivations, your deepest thoughts, your basic attitudes.

Available at your Christian bookstore or

STANDARD PUBLISHING